TIN GOOSE
The Fabulous Ford Trimotor

DEDICATED TO
Maude Valencia Conkling, my wonderful aunt, who raised me since I was six months old, and the only "Mother" I have ever known.

TIN GOOSE

The Fabulous Ford Trimotor

by Douglas J. Ingells

with Ralph Dietrick

Aero Publishers, Inc. • FALLBROOK, CALIFORNIA

ISBN-0-8168-8975-9

LIBRARY OF CONGRESS CATALOG CARD NUMBER 68-31759
COPYRIGHT© 1968 AERO PUBLISHERS, INC.
ALL RIGHTS RESERVED
PRINTED IN THE UNITED STATES OF AMERICA

PREFACE

June 1, 1968
Dearborn Inn
Greenfield Village
Dearborn, Michigan

ONE man did more, perhaps, than any other individual to get America rolling in the 20th Century. His name was Henry Ford whose inventiveness and ingenuity made the "horseless carriage" a practical motor car, and put the nation on wheels.

Mr. Ford did not invent the automobile. But with his famous Model-T "Tin Lizzie" which he put into mass production, he made it possible for tens of millions of persons to afford the luxury of inexpensive automobile transportation. With the advent of the Model-T, public demand brought into being the first system of paved roads and highways. The motor car changed the face of America and the habits, at work or play, of the nation's populace.

Much has been written of Mr. Ford's contribution to the world of wheels, but little is known of his farsightedness, encouragement and financial support to the world of wings. Yet, at a time when the aeroplane was regarded by most people as a noisey, bothersome winged intruder on society belonging to the dare-devil aviator, the gypsy flyer of the "roaring twenties," Mr. Ford saw in this machine a whole new concept in transportation for everyone.

It is said he took the airplane out of the cow pasture, put it in the hangar and gave aviation prestige and public confidence which launched the Air Age. In the midtwenties it was Mr. Ford who brought into production the first all-metal, high-wing, trimotor passenger transport planes. Affectionately, pilots called the Ford trimotor, the "Tin Goose" and the thundering, lumbering planes pioneered virtually every phase of present day air travel — from the ground up.

The "Tin Goose" by virtue of its metallic construction, trio of powerful engines, commodious interior and enormous wing had the look of security and safety. With the FORD name on it public acceptance was assured. Overnight, it became the most sought-after transport for the struggling family of privately-owned airlines born in the 1920's and early 1930's.

The "Goose" could land in unbelievingly small fields which helped provide air transportation to less populated communities, the beginnings of an airline network linking together big cities and small towns. Moreover, the plane could carry a good payload of passengers and mail at speeds of 100-mph, faster than any other form of transport. For a time, the Ford trimotors were the "sky queens," setting enviable records for time-table reliability and safety.

With the big trimotors Mr. Ford inaugurated the first regularly scheduled air mail service in the U.S. operated by a private company. The Ford Motor Company started the first air-freight operation between its Dearborn plant and factory branches in Chicago and Cleveland, the interiors of the planes stripped down to carry Model-T parts.

Aboard the planes on his own inter-company airline, Ford Air Transport Service, the first in-flight steward service was started with a "Flight Escort" as part of the crew. Pilots wore snappy uniforms to join the bus driver and the streetcar motorman as public chauffeurs in a common carrier.

On the ground at Dearborn, Ford built one of the finest airports of its time anywhere complete with paved runways, passenger terminal building, restaurant, hotel accommodations, radio communications shack, weather bureau, even a traffic control center. The airport could also accommodate lighter-than-air craft and the rigid dirigibles of the period, having the only privately-owned mooring mast in the country. It was here, too, that Ford started and sponsored the Reliability Air Tours which did for aviation what the famous Glidden Tours earlier had done for the automobile.

The "Tin Goose" brought it into being.

This, then, is her story, and the remarkable thing is that forty years after the first of her breed rolled out of the factory at Dearborn, she is still flying.

In 1928 I flew in one of the first Ford trimotors from Grand Rapids to Detroit, Michigan. Since that time I have probed through thousands of pictures and hundreds of reports at the Ford Archives in the Ford Museum near here. I have flown in seven of the remaining twelve flyable Fords. I have talked with pilots who flew the planes when they ruled the airlanes, and with mechanics who maintained them.

How the planes were born — How Mr. Ford got interested in aviation — The fabulous trimotors, themselves, and their exploits through the years — Why Mr. Ford stopped building the planes — All of this is a part of the Saga of The Tin Goose.

I have tried to record it here in narrative form.

More than just a story, the "Tin Goose" is a living legend about the beginnings of the greatest scheduled air transportation system in the world.

Douglas J. Ingells

ACKNOWLEDGEMENTS

The author is indebted to many individuals and organizations for helping in the preparation of this book.

I would particularly like to thank Mr. Ralph Dietrick and all the "gang" at Island Airlines for their cooperation and the many hours of flying in the "Tin Goose." Certainly more than any other individual, my friend Ralph Dietrick, president of Sky Tours, Inc. of Port Clinton, Ohio, inspired and encouraged, and made possible my taking the time to write the book. It is truly as much his book as it is mine.

Two others who helped immeasurably, giving freely of their time, were Mr. Henry Edmunds, Archivest at the Ford Archives, Greenfield Village, and Mr. Wynn Sears, his assistant. They were most cooperative in helping me to get the desired photographs and data about the early days of the Stout Metal Airplane Company and the Ford Motor Company aviation activities.

I am also grateful to the public relations people of Trans World Airlines, Northwest Orient Airlines, American Airlines, and Greenfield Village for their cooperation. Jack Hughes of Johnson Flying Service was also most helpful in supplying background and pictures.

Thanks also to Mr. Gaylord "Mox" Moxon of Moxon Electronics Corp. and Mox-Air, Inc. for his anecdotes and pictures, and for the flight in the most beautiful "Tin Goose" of all. For early background on the island airline operation, I am indebted to Milton "Red" Hershberger who started Island Air Service in 1929.

Then there is Betty Reed, who typed this manuscript so many times she knows the story better than anyone else.

Both the publishers and I also wish to thank William Winter, publisher & editor of *American Aircraft Modeler* magazine for permission to use material and photographs from the story "Cry Of The Tin Goose" appearing in that publication.

One other person, whose time and talent deserves recognition is my friend, Jim Goulet, owner of The Ludington Photographic Center & Studio, Ludington, Michigan. Jim spent many hours at the Ford Archives copying photographs from the original print collection pertaining to early history of the Ford Trimotors.

D.J.I

TABLE OF CONTENTS

Chapter
1 The Planes that Stout Built 9
2 Henry Ford and the Air Age 19
3 Those Fabulous Flying Fords 37
4 Island Home of the "Tin Goose" 59
5 The Second Time Around 78
   Index 95

IN 1927, three months before Charles A. Lindbergh made his epoch solo flight from New York to Paris, the Stout Metal Airplane Company produced the first of the all-metal, trimotors which pilots fondly called the "Tin Goose." Shown here is one of the first enclosed cockpit models to come off the assembly line. Actually Stout had little to do with the finalized configuration, and when this picture was taken Henry Ford had bought out the original Stout Metal Airplane Company. Today more than 40 years later, some of the old Ford trimotors are still flying. (Ford Archives Photo)

CHAPTER ONE

The Planes That Stout Built

BACK in 1923, Edsel Ford who was virtually running his father's vast automobile empire, The Ford Motor Company, received a most unusual letter. One paragraph read — *"I should like a thousand dollars, and I can only promise you one thing. You'll never see the money again!"*

The letter was signed — WILLIAM B. STOUT, inventor.

Young Ford, normally, would have thrown the letter in the waste basket along with thousands of similar requests he received from crackpots who wanted money for some crazy idea. But in this case, he didn't. Instead, he answered the letter, not only enclosing his own personal check for $1,000, but also a check for the same amount from his famous father.

Significantly, Edsel's decision thrust the biggest automobile manufacturer in the world precociously into the fledgling aviation industry. Within three years Ford was building a safe, all-metal transport plane, operating his own freight and passenger airline, flying the first commercial air mail, and the Ford name, alone, connected with flying started a revolution and evolution in the world of wings.

It is said, he took the airplane away from the "Barnstormer" and made the businessman aware of its potential as a new mode of transportation. If Henry Ford was interested, so was Wall Street. The result was that aviation got a blood transfusion, prestige and financial backing. Ford planes generated interest in building highways across the skies, just as the Model-T in another era had road-mapped the United States. The wing joined the wheel in the movement of people and things to change the way we think and act and do business together as individuals and nations.

II

ONE reason, perhaps, why Edsel Ford answered Bill Stout's "fund-raising" letter was because he had heard of the inventor and was well aware of Stout's reputation. William Bushnell Stout (close friends called him "Jackknife") was the grandson of David Bushnell, who is credited with developing the first submarine

William Bushnell Stout, who interested Henry Ford in building all-metal transport planes. Stout is standing in front of his experimental design called the "Aerial Sedan."
(Ford Archives Photo)

9

In 1918-19, Stout Engineering Laboratories produced this metal and plywood aircraft nick-named "The Vampire Bat."
(Ford Archives Photo)

during the Revolutionary War. Minnesota-born Bill Stout was a kind of Buster Brown in aviation circles. He got interested in aeronautics when he saw Glenn Curtiss fly his famous "June Bug" during an exhibition at St. Paul in 1910. Curtiss inspired Stout to make aviation his career. Stout attended the University of Minnesota, picking up a background in both journalism and engineering. Out of college for a while he covered the aviation beat for the Chicago *Tribune*, then founded and edited his own aviation magazine *Aerial Age,* one of the first of the aviation trade publications.

But Stout was restless, full of ideas and dreams, and he wanted to try them out. He gave up journalism to become a journeyman with the Scripps-Booth Motor Company of Detroit, helping to build bicycles and automobiles. During World War I, Stout was hired by Alvan Macauley to work for Packard, where he got well acquainted with the famous Liberty engine and the U.S.-built DeHaviland (DH-4) warplanes. Later, Howard Coffin, head of the Wartime Aircraft Production Board took him on as an advisor. It was probably during this period that both Fords first heard the name Bill Stout. There was close inter-relationship between the automotive industry and the war-born, rapidly expanding aircraft production program.

During the Great War and the period right after the Armistice in 1918, Stout took a good look at the shortcomings of various aircraft designs. He concluded, that most of these planes, with their cloth and wood construction and the maze of struts and wire bracings, were structurally unsound and aerodynamically impractical.

Stout decided to do something about it. He had heard of the famous Junkers firm in Germany that was building planes of all-metal construction with cantilever-type wings, no external bracing. With his own money, he designed and built a radically-shaped aircraft that in configuration looked like a vampire bat. Of wood construction, it was covered with thin veneer instead of fabric, and its outstanding feature was a thick wing. There were no wires or struts. He talked C. W. "Charlie" Nash, the rebel of the automotive world, into giving him a 150-horsepower Hispano-Suiza engine, and the so-called "Bat Wing" made a successful flight.

That was in 1920, and "The Bat" was so impressive, Stout interested R. L. Stranahan, president of the Champion Spark Plug Company in putting up some money to start Stout Engineering Laboratories and "further explore the design potential." The following year Stout built a greatly improved "Bat Wing" and Bert ("Give me

Stout's "batwing" design was one of first planes in this country to employ the principle of the cantilever wing. This is Bat No. 2 (top) during unique strength test in factory. Stout figures that if the weight of ten men (count them) couldn't break the wing, it was safe. In middle photo, note the large spinner on propeller and radiators which were retractable, "streamling" ideas far in advance of the period. Below, one can easily see resemblence to "Vampire Bat." (Ford Archives Photo)

In 1922 Stout got contract from U. S. Navy to build a twin-engined, all-metal torpedo bomber. The design, shown here, was one of first planes in this country to use corrugated metal construction.

(Ford Archives Photo)

enough horsepower, and I'll fly a barn door!") Acosta, test pilot and record-smasher, took the plane up on its first flight. Resultant publicity got the U. S. Navy interested. The Navy commissioned Stout to design and build a twin-engined torpedo plane.

In its construction Stout used metal instead of wood for the first time. There are some claims to the contrary, but little proof, that it wasn't the first all-metal aircraft built in the United States. One thing is certain, Stout strongly advocated all-metal construction for aircraft, and he pioneered many metal-forming techniques. The Navy "Bat", however, met with disaster. One of the Navy's own test pilots cracked it up. The plane was a total wreck, and the Navy rejected the design. Stout lost over $150,000 in the venture.

"The bluest day of my career," he wrote later.

The truth is, it was probably the luckiest day in his life. The misfortune led him to write his now famous letter which he sent to a hundred or more prominent businessmen and industrialists. Stout, himself, admitted he was "through with government

The Navy torpedo bomber because of its enormous wing area was also called "The Bat." Plane crashed shortly after this picture was taken and Navy lost interest. *(Ford Archives Photo)*

red-tape" and so turned to private industry to further his aviation career.

The letter often misquoted, did include the "guarantee" that investors would probably never see their $1000 again, but it also offered a *service* which Stout was certainly capable of providing. Bill Stout, turned writer/editor again, offered the select group a weekly newsletter explaining the fundamentals of aviation. In a short time, he raised over $125,000, the initial capital with which he started the Stout Metal Airplane Company in Dearborn, Michigan.

Recalling that letter, Stout in later years, confided that it opened the door for him to personally meet with many farsighted, influential individuals, and convince them of the great potential of the air age. During these interviews he sold the idea for a new, radically-designed transport plane employing the cantilever wing and built entirely of duralumin, a new light weight metal of super strength.

The list of "angels" who helped him get started reads like a Who's Who of American millionaires and free-enterprisers — The Fisher Brothers (body builders for GM), Walter P. Chrysler, J. G. Vincent (of Liberty-Engine fame), Harold Pitcairn (pioneer airline operator, the father of the autogiro in the United States), R. E. Olds (Oldsmobile), Harvey Firestone, C. F. "Boss" Kettering and W. S. "Bill" Knudsen (General Motors), Marshall Field, William F. Scripps, Earl Holley, Roy D. Chapin, Albert Champion, Gar Wood, Alex Dow, Phillip K. Wrigley, B. F. Everitt, William E. Metzger, R. L. Polk, Horace E. Dodge, Arthur H. Buhl, E. L. Claxton, C. S. Mott, Joseph Boyer and E. D. Stair.

There were others. But heading the list — and, perhaps, the "lever" Stout used in gaining such interest and support from so select and influential an audience were two names — HENRY and EDSEL FORD.

The Ford-Stout relationship, to say the least, was a strange one. At best, Ford liked Stout because the man in some ways demonstrated the spark of genius; he was full of ideas, and he was very much an eccentric. Perhaps, in these traits, Henry Ford saw himself in the mirror. But, beyond this, the relationship broke down. Ford never took Stout into his inner circle,

Henry Ford (left) and Bill Stout. This is one of the rare photographs taken of the two men during the early design and development stages of the first single-engined Stout "Air Pullman" and "Air Transport" planes. (Ford Archives Photo)

and, sometimes, he indicated he would like to get rid of the man for keeps. He saw in Stout more of a promotor than an engineer, which proved true. Yet, for some reason, the billionaire never objected to Stout using the Ford name to further his own interests. In aviation, Stout took full advantage of the opportunity.

There is no question Ford money helped Stout in the manufacturing end of the aviation business. The Stout Metal Airplane Company was just the beginning.

III

THE first project for the newly formed Stout Metal Airplane Company was the building of a four-place, plywood and fabric monoplane that Bill Stout called the *"Air Sedan."* The plane was powered with a Curtiss OX-5, ninety-horsepower motor. It employed the principle of the cantilever, wing, but the machine was grossly underpowered for its weight and design configuration. Nothing much ever came of

Stout's first attempt at a transport plane was this "Aerial Sedan" model produced by newly formed Stout Metal Airplane Company. Plane was built of plywood and metal construction, and powered with Curtiss OX-5 engine. Note that Stout still favored "bat wing" configuration. (Ford Archives Photo)

it. Stout himself confessed that he tried to get a 150-horsepower Hispano Suiza engine to overcome the plane's power deficiency, but the Hissos were in scarce supply, so he abandoned the project. In another version of the *"Air Sedan,"* mostly of all-metal construction, he did try the more powerful engine. The *"Air Sedan"* did fly. But the Stout Metal Airplane Company was running out of money.

Then, something happened. One day, during flight tests of the "Air Sedan" at Selfridge Field, an Army Air Corps base near Mount Clemens, Michigan, Henry Ford and Edsel came to see the performance. Nobody got real excited over the test results, but Henry Ford remarked to Edsel — "I think this fellow is on the right track."

Stout, overhearing the statement and

Improved version of the "Aerial Sedan" became this "Air Sedan" of all-metal construction. Plane was tested at Selfridge Field, Army Air Corps base, where Henry and Edsel Ford witnessed trials. Both Fords were so impressed that they put more money into the struggling Stout Metal Airplane Company.
(Ford Archives Photo)

seeing a twinkle in Henry Ford's eyes, promptly took advantage of the situation. "Mister Ford," he said, "this thing isn't worth a damn. I need more horsepower. To get it, I need more money..."

Henry Ford took another glance at the plane. Then he turned to Stout and said: "You don't need more money, son. You need more airplane!" The Fords came up with more development money.

Stout already had the bigger plane on paper. It was an all-metal, high-wing design built around the Liberty engine and capable of carrying eight passengers. He called it the "Air Pullman" and Walter Lees, a famous test pilot flew the plane in a series of some 300 tests at Selfridge.

The single engined "Air Pullman" was one of the most rugged airplanes ever built to date. During the National Air Races of 1924 held at Dayton, Ohio, the plane was used to shuttle VIP's back and forth between Detroit and Dayton. On one trip, with Eddie Stinson at the controls, trouble developed in a faulty fuel line, and the engine caught fire.

Stinson cut the switch, and put his flying skill to test. He fanned out the flames "side-slipping", and then, put the plane down in a farmer's field. Nobody was hurt. The crash landing paid big dividends for Stout.

On board the plane that day was Professor E. P. Warner of the Massachusetts

Bill Stout in mock-up of first "Air Pullman" which was sponsored primarily by Ford, the true beginning of Henry Ford's entry into the air transport field. (Ford Archives Photo)

Institute of Technology. Warner had been commissioned by the Post Office Department to make a survey of various aircraft types that might be suitable for flying the mail. He was so impressed by the "Air

The first "Air Pullman" on initial test flight from Selfridge Field.   (Ford Archives Photo)

15

The first of the "Air Transport" (2-AT series) takes shape in the Stout Metal Airplane Company factory. Plane was later christened "Maiden Dearborn" and would play leading role in establishment of Ford Air Transport Service, first privately-owned, scheduled airline in U.S. (Ford Archives Photo)

Pullman's" performance and its inherent structural safety features, that he recommended that the Post Office buy one.

The order came through. But to build another plane, Stout had to seek further financial help. At the time, he couldn't even meet his small company's payroll. He turned to Henry and Edsel Ford, hoping they would come to the rescue.

Henry Ford called in his chief engineer, William B. Mayo. "What do you think of this thing?" the father of the Model-T asked.

Mayo glanced over at Edsel, who was also in on the conference. Edsel nodded. Then, Mayo answered his boss — "He's already got more than $5,000 of my money, too!"

Edsel had talked Bill Mayo into putting money into the Stout Metal Airplane Company months before. Relying on Mayo's judgement, Henry Ford gave the green light, and Stout walked out of the office that day with a package deal that spelled only progress.

In the *Ford News,* a company publication, dated July 15, 1924 there appeared an announcement that was to have far-reaching import on aviation.

The item said: *"For the purpose of encouraging aircraft development the Ford interests will erect a modern factory building devoted to research in aviation. The building will be used by the Stout Metal Airplane Company and the Aircraft Development Corp."*

The factory was to be located on a 600-acre site that Ford owned, and in summer

The Stout approach to an all-metal trimotor was this 3-AT "Air Pullman" which was later destroyed by fire. Features which appear later in the Ford-built "Tin Goose" trimotors are the thick, corrugated, cantilever wing, vertical fin and rudder and aft cabin section of fuselage. Mounting of engine in the wing was far ahead of the period. (Ford Archives Photo)

of 1924 Fordson tractors cleared a tract of land and construction was started.

IV

MEANWHILE, Stout went to work on another project which, essentially, was a modified version of the "Air Pullman", called the "Air Transport", produced under Ford sponsorship. This plane was the first of those that Stout built to have the familiar FORD emblem on its fuselage. It was also designated the 2-AT (because it was the second model-type of the air transport series) and Ford was greatly impressed with the plane and its performance.

Ford gave Stout an order for five of the planes. He also made it known that he planned to use these planes to start a company-owned airline to carry freight and personnel between the main Ford plant in Dearborn and factory branches in Chicago and Cleveland. Moreover, he revealed that he planned to surround the new factory site with a modern airport and terminal facilities to further the development of the airplane and the airport would materialize much sooner than anyone expected.

Henry Ford, however, did not want to stop with the "Air Transport" design. He wanted a larger plane and he told Stout to do something about it.

Stout tried putting three of the Liberty engines on a new "Air Pullman" of radical design. He had an aversion for the name, probably because he had at one time designed a self-propelled, lightweight railroad Pullman car. It never amounted to much. Neither did the Liberty-powered "Air Pullman" and the project was abandoned at an early stage.

But the trimotor "Air Pullman" was revived again using the latest Wright, radial, air-cooled engines. Designated the 3-AT, the plane's performance was disappointing, as we shall see in the next chapter. The 3-AT did, however, have its place in aviation history. The plane was the last that Stout designed for Ford, and their relationship "cooled" from that time forward.

It must also be mentioned that because Stout had designed the 3-AT, and because Ford sponsored this original trimotor, the popular version of the Ford/Stout story is that Stout designed the famous Ford trimotors, the "Tin Goose", as pilots affectionately called them.

The facts tell us a different story, exploding one of aviation's greatest myths since Edgar Allen Poe fabricated his great hoax about a balloon crossing the Atlantic in 1884. Poe's fictional heroes did NOT make the crossing, and Bill Stout did NOT design the "Tin Goose" in the configuration that we know it today.

The Edsel Ford/Van Auken aeroplane built in 1909, six years after the Wright Brothers' first success at Kitty Hawk, N.C. It was probably Henry Ford's first interest in flying machines, generated by Edsel's request to help his childhood friend Van Auken with the project. Unique feature is tricycle landing gear, probably the first of its kind. Pilot is believed to be Van Auken. (Ford Archives Photo)

CHAPTER TWO

Henry Ford And The Air Age

HENRY FORD did not invent the automobile. In 1769 Nicholas Cugnot, a Frenchman, made the first "road wagon", a three-wheeled, self-propelled, steam-powered vehicle. And in 1875, another Frenchman, Etienne Lenoir, produced the first carriage-type mobile employing the internal combustion engine. Seldon, Krebs, Duryea and others, progressively worked to develop the "horseless carriage" as we know it today. But it was Henry Ford who gave the idea practicability, put the motor car into mass production, and is generally credited with putting the nation on wheels.

There is a strange parallel in aviation. Ford did not invent the airplane. The Wright Brothers did. But Ford pioneered many aviation firsts that built public confidence in air transportation and put the world on wings. His contribution was far more than just financial support in the development of the all-metal "Air Transport" and the first Ford trimotors. Ford took a look at the whole sphere of influence which the fledgling aircraft industry was creating a guess-and-by-God fashion, and then, drew up his own blueprint for the future.

It was Bill Stout's claim before his death in 1956, that his greatest contribution to aviation was getting Henry Ford interested in it. Certainly, Stout did excite Ford's interest and progress was the result. But Henry Ford was interested in the field of aeronautics long before the two ever met, and *before* Edsel received Stout's now famous letter.

Edsel was a boy of fifteen, when he went to his father and said he wanted support to help build a flying machine. A youth by the name of Charles Van Auken had excited Edsel about the project, and Edsel had helped him research for information on the design of aero vehicles. There were two others, William Theisen and James Smith, who were also in on the project.

The older Ford, wanting to push Edsel into anything mechanical, agreed to help, and rented a barn to the rear of 1302 Woodward Avenue in Detroit. Historically, this became the first Ford aircraft factory, although it was really just a place where the boys could work. Most of the machine work was done at the Piquette plant of the Ford Motor Company. Nevertheless, the barn was the birthplace of the first Ford airplane in 1909 — only six years after the Wright Brothers flew the first man-carrying, power-driven machine at Kitty Hawk, North Carolina.

When the boys had finished their project, what emerged from the barn was a single-place, high-wing monoplane of wood, metal, fabric and glue construction, and held together by struts and wires. It was powered with a direct drive Model-T engine developing 28 horsepower. Interestingly, and certainly far ahead of its time, the craft rested on a tricycle landing gear!

The controls were conventional-type rudder, ailerons and elevators. But the operator wore a yoke around his shoulders, and by shifting to the right or left, he controlled the movement of the ailerons. It was a similar principle used earlier by the Wrights in their first experiments with the power-driven machine. In the Ford airplane, however, the operator sat in an upright position. The Wrights' lay prone on the lower wing.

The Edsel/Van Auken plane did fly. It made its first flight from a Ford-owned farm on the site of what now is the Dear-

The 1909 Ford/Van Auken "flyer" was powered with a souped-up Model-T direct-drive engine developing 28-horsepower. Plane never did get more than a few feet off the ground.
(Ford Archives Photo)

born Country Club. In the beginning, they had trouble because the machine was underpowered. A souped-up Model-T engine helped, and Van Auken made several flights that attracted considerable attention.

Later the plane was hauled to the site of historic old Fort Wayne near Detroit where demonstration trials were conducted from the Fort's parade ground. Edsel never flew in the plane. The plane barely got off the ground in its attempt to fly, but it did excite much interest among the spectators who came to see the show. Subsequently, the machine was smashed beyond repair, and Edsel lost interest. So did Henry Ford, probably influenced by the spectacular success of the Wright Brothers' machine at the Army trials in Fort Myer, Virginia about the same time.

Edsel's experiment is noted here, however, because it definitely shows Henry Ford's first interest in the flying machine. That interest was revived during World War I when the Ford Motor Company helped produce the famous Liberty engines for America's great Air Armada promised to her allies.

Although he was making engines for the American-built DeHavilland warplanes, Ford, himself, didn't particularly like the idea. He called the airplane — "one of those damned war-making machines."

It was not until he saw what Stout was doing with his passenger-carrying transport designs, that Ford began to see the airplane in a different light.

On one occasion Ford talked to a Detroit newspaperman and explained — "The airplane is going to enlarge the work of the automobile. The motor car has mixed people up so thoroughly that one can hardly fool any American anymore about any part of his own country. But they can be fooled about other parts of the world. The airplane will stop that. In a motor car you can go almost anywhere land exists. In an airplane you can go almost anywhere a man can breathe. And with the development of the supercharger it is possible to go places even where man cannot breathe under normal circumstances . . . When the plane becomes popular, it will put power into peoples' hands just as the motor car has. And when international financiers or politicians propose a war, the people will know why, and ask a lot of questions. They will make short work of these war-makers."

Henry Ford's theory about the airplane and its "peace potential" made front pages all over the country. Here, perhaps, was the real reason Henry Ford got into aviation to the extent that he did. Surely, there must have been something stronger than just another business venture. Ford, himself, wasn't convinced of the safety of airplanes. He said so publicly. He was build-

Edsel Ford, who took an interest in Bill Stout's activities and talked his father into backing the Stout Metal Airplane Company.
(Ford Archives Photo)

The first two production models of the Liberty-powered, single-engined "Air Transport".
(Ford Archives Photo)

ing planes and operating an airline before he ever made a flight in a plane. Lindbergh, after his epoch flight to Paris in 1927, took Ford up for his first plane ride. Ford seldom flew after that. Yet, another item in the *Ford News*, dated August 8, 1925, quoted Henry Ford as saying — "There seems to be a wonderful future in aviation. So we are going to build the best planes we can, and if it does develop we will be ready!"

II

THE first Stout Metal Airplane Company factory on Ford property near Dearborn was just the beginning. It was there the single-engined, Liberty-powered, "Air Transports" were born. Ford paid $22,500 for the first of these planes; $20,000 a piece for the others, and almost immediately he started thinking of putting them to work.

One day in April, 1925, Ford met Bill Stout in the hall of the Ford Laboratory. "I've been thinking about an air service to Chicago," he told Stout. "How soon can we start?"

Stout was caught off guard. He had been having engine trouble with the first model 2-AT, just completed. Tests had worn out the engine. For a minute he hesitated to answer.

Ford pressured him: "This is Saturday. Can we start it Monday?"

Stout shook his head. "That's impossible," he explained. "The plane needs a new engine."

Henry Ford frowned, started to walk away.

"We can start it a week from Monday," Stout shouted after him.

So it was, that on Monday April 13, 1925, there was much activity on the ramp in front of the Stout Metal Airplane Factory with its adjacent flying field which had been dedicated on January 15 the same year, and appropriately named Ford Airport. The Stout-built 2-AT "Air Transport," *"Maiden Dearborn I"*, took off loaded with 1300 pounds of auto parts for the Chicago Ford plant. The plane's destination was another Ford-owned airfield and hangar at Lansing, Illinois, about 25 miles southeast of Chicago. A short time later the plane landed, right on time, and the world's first regularly scheduled airline, devoted solely to the business of one company was born. Henry Ford was pioneering again.

In the beginning, the schedule called for one flight a day in each direction. Westbound, the plane left Detroit at 3:15 P. M., arrived in Chicago at 5:00 P. M. Eastbound, it left Chicago at 8:00 A. M. and arrived in Detroit at 11:40 that morning. The service was daily, and Henry Ford, himself, kept a close watch on the timetable reliability.

Once, Edsel Ford was 20 minutes late trying to make the Chicago plane. When he got to the airport, the plane was gone.

"This is an airline, not a yacht," his father told him.

On July 1, 1925, the new air service was expanded including more daily flights. Cleveland was added to the schedule. A plane left Detroit at 10:40 a.m. daily, arriving Cleveland at 12:15 p.m. Westbound, the schedule called for departure Cleveland at 2:30 p.m., arriving Detroit at 4:05 p.m. Right from the start the airline operation was a success.

Back and forth between the three terminals — Chicago-Detroit-Cleveland — the planes shuttled parts, mail and personnel. The Ford Air Transport Service set an enviable record.

On the anniversary of its first full year of operation Bill Stout had this to say: "The entire year of flying has been accomplished without a single injury to anyone and with a remarkable freedom from mechanical trouble. Over 1,000 trips have been made, and a distance covered equal to ten times around the world at speeds close to one hundred miles an hour. This has been done without any blowing of trumpets, but just as an everyday, routine, transportation proposition. Practically no changes have been made in the planes which are the same today as in the beginning. That the maintenance is simple, is proved by the fact that the two airlines have been run with only four airplanes, this including three trips a day on the Chicago route and two a day on the Cleveland run, with the planes running in each direction carrying 1,000 to 1,500 pounds in passengers and freight on every trip."

Ford's airline had also done much more than just perform a vitally important transportation service and prove the value of scheduled airline operation. At Henry Ford's insistance Ford pilots wore snappy blue and gold uniforms, "because it gives dignity to their profession." He also instigated a "Flight Escort" service aboard the planes.

The "Flight Escort" was a uniformed attendant, who went along on each flight to make passengers comfortable, and explain to them the functions of the airline and points of scenic interest along the route.

The Ford Air Transport Service had been in operation less than three months when the Post Office Department, under the Air Mail Act of 1925, announced it was going to turn the operation of the Air Mail over to private contractors. The announcement said any company engaged in operating an air service could take part in the bids for carrying the mail.

This fleet of Ford single-engined "Air Transports" (the famous 2-AT series) flew over 1,000 trips between Detroit-Chicago-Cleveland during first year of operations of the Ford Air Transport Service. Most of these planes were later sold to Florida Airways, a predecessor company of today's Eastern Airlines.
(Ford Archives Photo)

Loading the first commercial air mail, February 15, 1926. Plane is 2-AT Ford/"Air Transport," and minutes later it took off for the inaugural Detroit-Chicago run. (Ford Archives Photo)

On September 8, 1925, the Postmaster General of the United States, Harry S. New, paid a visit to Detroit for a talk with Henry Ford. It was a significant and convenient visit. The Postmaster General in so many words told Henry Ford he wanted him to bid for the Detroit-Chicago and Detroit-Cleveland routes which were to become CAM-6 and CAM-7, among the first Contract Air Mail Routes. It was logical that Ford, who had more experience and more equipment to do the job in this area than anyone else, should get the contract. And he did.

The Ford Air Transport Service, became the first private contractor to fly the U.S. Air Mail. On February 15, 1926 Captain Lawrence (Larry) G. Fritz, and Captains Ross Kirkpatrick and Dean Burford, Ford pilots, started the service over the new routes. Fritz took off first in one of the liberty-powered "Air Transports" eastward for Cleveland. Then, Kirkpatrick lifted another of the planes into the sky from Ford Airport, and pointed its nose for Chicago. On the lakefront at Chicago's airport, Burford took off about the same time and headed for Detroit.

Commercial Air Mail was inaugurated that day.

At Ford Airport for the inaugural ceremonies was Second Assistant Postmaster General, W. Irving Glover, who made a speech over a national radio hook-up. "To Mr. Ford goes the honor of being the first to undertake this new type of mail transport," Glover declared. "It is really a first step in a new epoch."

Henry Ford replied — "I sent a letter on the first mail plane to my friend Thomas Edison in which I told him, I thought this was a great step forward."

He added: "The pioneering in plane building and operation is past. It now remains for men of business to take hold of the opportunity."

III

PERHAPS, more than anyone else, Henry Ford took advantage of every opportunity to push progress in virtually every phase of aviation — from the ground up. He had definite ideas as to what he wanted. These ideas, undoubtedly, must have conflicted with those of Bill Stout because on July 31, 1925 — the day after his 62nd birthday anniversary — Henry Ford bought out the stock and assets of Stout Metal Airplane Com-

Many efforts were made to improve the 2-AT's performance. Stout even tried powering the "Air Transport" with the new Wright "Whirlwind," radial, air-cooled engine. The project was abandoned when Ford began encouraging development of trimotor configuration. (Ford Archives Photo)

pany. Ford paid two dollars for every dollar invested by the other stockholders. The small factory closed down the same day for inventory.

When the factory opened again three days later, William Benson Mayo, nominal chief engineer of the Ford Motor Company was in charge, although Stout remained on the payroll. Significantly, the Ford Motor Company had become a full-fledged member of the aircraft manufacturing community.

From the beginning, the Ford influence was felt. Even though, he admitted, the Ford Air Transport Service airline was doing much better than he had expected, Ford still wasn't satisfied with the 2-AT "Air Transport" planes. It was at this point, that Ford told Stout to "go ahead" with the 3-AT, Wright-powered "Air Pullman" trimotor.

When the plane emerged from the factory, some observers called it a "mechanical monstrosity." Aerodynamically, it was almost absurd. The outboard engines mounted in the wings with little or no streamlining, virtually destroyed the flight characteristics of the airfoil. It had an open-cockpit mounted on top of the wing, which only added to the airflow problems. The forward section of the fuselage looked like a dirigible's gondola car. The third engine, mounted in front and below the cabin window line, appeared to be "something, somebody just added at the last minute." But it was a bigger plane than the "Air Transport," and it did fly.

To run his airline, Ford hired Major R. W. "Shorty" Schroeder, an Army flier of high-altitude record fame, and one crisp day in November, 1925, Schroeder took the 3-AT aloft on its initial flight. He was Ford's chief test pilot.

Henry Ford and his "top brass" turned out to see the test. They saw the plane roar into the sky in a fairly normal take-off, and everybody was all smiles. But almost immediately, Schroeder started to come down for a landing. The plane dropped like a brick from about thirty feet, bounced up

The first Stout trimotor, the 3-AT, showing close-up frontal view of engines in wings and gondola-shaped fuselage. Ford called it a "monstrosity." Note very little resemblance to ultimate Ford "Tin Goose" design.
(Ford Archives Photo)

Stout's 3-AT "Air Pullman" experimental trimotor in flight. The plane did fly, but not very well, and test pilot reports threw a wet blanket on the whole project. There was only one 3-AT ever built.

(Ford Archives Photos)

that high again, repeated the yo-yo action, and then, its pilot gunned the motors wide-open and climbed. He circled the field, and the next time made a successful landing with plenty of power, not the normal procedure. Schroeder told Ford to "forget it."

Later, another pilot flew the plane. A time-worn copy of his report says in part . . . "It would be commercially impossible to operate this plane with a payload of 800 pounds . . . the weight of four passengers and baggage . . . With a 1500 pound payload this airplane will not fly level on two motors (to meet Ford's envisioned safety requirement) and it was not considered safe to land the airplane even on as large a field as the Ford Airport with the three engines functioning perfectly . . ."

Henry Ford was disgusted. He paid little attention to what anyone did with the 3-AT after the disappointing performance. Then, one night in January, 1926, a mysterious fire completely gutted the Stout Metal Airplane Company factory.

According to Tom Towle, one of the aeronautical engineers who had worked with Stout — "The only trace of the 3 or 4 airplanes (inside the factory at the time of the fire) were the steel parts on the floor in all of their correct relative positions. My own opinion was that much gasoline was used in the fire, and the heat was so intense there was left not a trace of aluminum. The floor was covered with gray ashes. Everyone at the factory was laid off indefinitely. There was little talk about the fire, but there was talk about who had the factory burned or why!

One thing was certain. The fire had completely destroyed the Stout version of what *never did become the famous "Tin Goose" Ford trimotor.*

"The day after the fire," Towle recalls, "Stout came to the empty south half of Ford's laboratory with a roll of craft paper, a hammer, glue and some sticks etc., and started to make a wood and paper mock-up on the floor near my lonesome drafting board. The mock-up indicated that what he had in mind was almost a duplicate of the 'Air Pullman' trimotor. Stout worked for a couple of hours and then left. Shortly thereafter, Bill Mayo appeared, alone, and told me to start immediately to design a three engine transport. Apparently, I assumed, the disappointing performance of the 3-AT had resulted in the decision by Bill Mayo and Mr. Ford to keep Stout out of airplane designing. I don't recall seeing Stout in Mr. Ford's laboratory after that."

Until some decision was reached about the future, Stout was told by Bill Mayo that Henry Ford wanted him to go on an extensive lecture tour around the country promoting aviation. More idea man, writer, and promoter than he was engineer, Stout was delighted with the opportunity. But before he left, he sent Ford some sketches and a new proposal for another trimotor design. It was, essentially, the "Air Pullman" all over again with some modifications and improvements. Nothing ever came of it.

Ford had a better idea. Harold Hicks, who had designed racing boats for Edsel, was made chief aviation engineer of a newly

"The Josephine Ford" plywood and cloth trimotor in which Commander Richard E. Byrd flew over the North Pole in 1926. Edsel Ford helped finance Byrd Polar expedition. Design is said to have influenced Ford in the final design configuration of the "Tin Goose." In the same view (insert) Island Airlines' Ford trimotor shows striking profile likeness.   (Ford Archives and Island Airlines photos)

formed Airplane Division of the Ford Motor Company. Tom Towle, for a while was the only other employee. But later, Hicks hired three young M.I.T. graduates, Otto Koppen, John Lee and James McDonnell (now chairman of the board and president of the McDonnell-Douglas Aircraft Co.) and put them to work on a "concept" for a trimotor that Henry Ford had in mind.

"I did the first three-view drawings," Towle declares, "employing a different wing and fuselage configuration. The others came along a little later and, working together, we came up with the finalized version of what was to become the 'Tin Goose' in its popular profile.

"By the time Stout returned from his lecture tour, things were too far along for him to have anything to say about it. The plane already was being built in the new factory."

Designated the 4-AT because it was the fourth model type of the "Air Transport" series, the design resembled the original Stout "Air Pullman" trimotor about as much as a pelican resembles a partridge. It did, however, look like a Chinese copy of the plywood-and-cloth trimotors designed by Anthony Hermann Gerhard Fokker, the Dutchman, who built World War I warplanes for the Kaiser. The trimotor Fokkers were making a name for themselves in the skies here at home and abroad.

Coincidentally, it was a Fokker trimotor that Commander Richard E. Byrd had selected for his planned flight over the North Pole. The plane was named "The Josephine Ford", after Edsel's wife, because Ford money helped to finance the 1925-26 Byrd expedition. The story goes, that both Fords, understandably, were "sold" on the Fokker's performance capabilities, and the word went down to Hicks to — "build one like that, only make it out of metal."

One thing is well substantiated, Bill Stout had very little to do with the ultimate Ford trimotor design, although for 40 years

Gander of the "Tin Goose" family was this 4-AT trimotor, first of Ford-engineered designs. Plane had open-cockpit, side-by-side seating for pilots. Note strange landing gear strut arrangement and mud fenders over wire-spoked wheels. Distinctive feature of future models was the square-shaped barn-door-like rudder. This picture was taken just before initial test flight. Ford, still skeptical, didn't even want his name on the experimental design. (Ford Archives Photo)

the popular version is that Stout designed the "Tin Goose."

The fact is, Bill Stout, whom this writer interviewed many times, never did claim he designed the "Tin Goose." He didn't say he didn't either, letting his listeners draw their own conclusions on the strength of his reputation and his known close association with the Ford Motor Company. The unfortunate thing is that Stout, who died in 1956, intentionally or unintentionally, never set the record straight. In his autobiography (*"So, Away I Went"* Bobbs-Merrill, 1947) Stout mentions only his work on the "Air Sedan", the original Liberty-powered "Air Pullman," the "Air Transport" and the "Air Pullman" trimotor. There isn't a single picture of the "Tin Goose" in the entire book and on some pages, the author in a cynical tone, criticizes the Ford-designed trimotor.

Stout did say, and he never let anyone forget it — "My greatest contribution was getting Henry Ford interested in building airplanes." That, alone, earned him a place in Aviation's Hall of Fame.

IV

THE first model 4-AT, the original "Tin Goose", was an open-cockpit job, but later this was changed and the pilot was given an enclosed cockpit, faired into the thick wing, part of the famous "turtle-back" that smoothed out airflow characteristics. Outboard engines were slung in a strut arrangement in cone-shaped nacelles under the wings, and aerodynamically, the 4-AT was a vastly improved design.

On June 11, 1926, Major Schroeder took the new plane up for its maiden flight.

Six months after first 4-AT completed tests, Ford had turned the factory into an assembly line for producing the planes. Here are some of first models moving into final assembly. Note different wing tip configuration and window and landing gear changes, enclosed cockpit. (Ford Archives Photo)

Everybody was more than pleased, and from that moment on a whole line of Ford Trimotors made aviation history.

There would be many versions, bigger, better, models with improved streamlining and more horsepower, but the basic design, like the Model-T, never lost its identity. Characteristic of Ford, he put the design on the assembly line. In the process, he pioneered many production techniques, shaping and forming into plane parts a new alloy called "Alclad" which combined the corrosion-resistance of pure aluminum with the strength of duralumin.

The raw material went in a back door of the factory, and finished planes, bright and shiny, emerged from the front which also served as a gigantic hangar. As fast as the planes saw daylight, they were rolled onto the ramp and test flown. Ford had turned the adjacent flying field into one of the most modern airports in the country. Its facilities far out-stripped those of any city of that period, and even today would be considered adequate for scheduled air service operations.

The landing area sprawled out over more than 600 acres of level ground. Two runways (one was 2,800-feet in length, the other 2,600 feet) criss-crossed each other to take advantage of winds that might blow from any direction. A large part of the runway surfaces were concrete — the first paved runways in the United States.

Next to the factory, along the same side of the airport's perimeter, were two other large hangars and maintenance shop facili-

*This is an aerial view of Ford Airport at Dearborn, Michigan in 1929. Field had paved runways, a terminal building, airport hotel, restaurant, weather observatory and mooring mast for dirigibles and lighter-than-aircraft. New Stout Metal Airplane Company factory (now part of Ford Motor Company) is in foreground. Ford never changed name of factory.
(Ford Archives Photo)*

The passenger terminal building at Ford Airport was one of first in the U.S. Ford also introduced airport taxi and airport bus service. Picture was taken after Ford Air Transport Service became Detroit-Cleveland Air Service. (Ford Archives Photo)

Interior view of Terminal Building at Ford Airport, Dearborn, Michigan. (Ford Archives Photo)

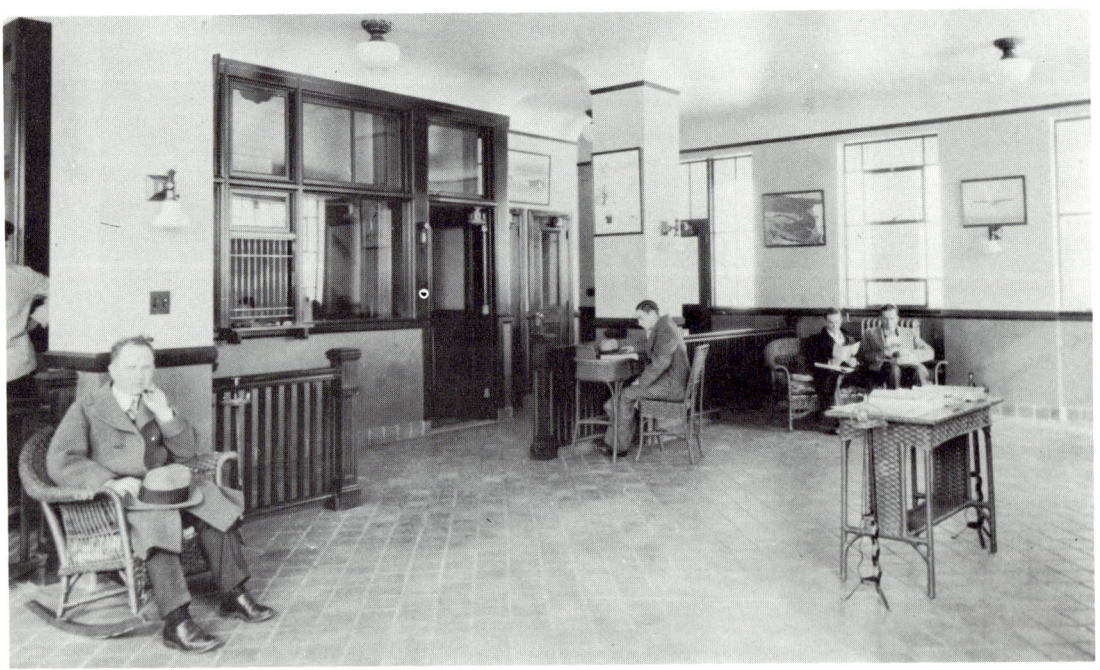

Navy's pride of the skies, the dirigible "Los Angeles" (left) at mooring mast, Ford Airport, the only privately-owned dirigible landing facility in the U.S. "Los Angeles" was frequent visitor. Photo at right shows Army blimp at mooring position. (Ford Archives Photo)

ties. These housed the Ford Air Transport Service planes. Both hangars and shops were available for transient aircraft as well. The airport was open to all fliers.

Atop the main hangar was a complete U.S. Weather Bureau Station where pilots could get up-to-the-minute weather information. Sandwiched between the hangars was a radio shack. Transmitters and receivers were in continuous operation. Ford had his own Traffic Control System for the airline operation. In addition, the first radio beacons, pioneered by Ford engineers, guided properly-equipped planes on a beeline direct to the Ford Airport from fifty miles out.

Near the main entrance to the airport was a low, square structure of white brick and stone — a modern passenger terminal complete with ticket counter, waiting room and esplanade where curious onlookers could watch flight operations. The terminal also had a fireplace. And there was a snack bar for hungry passengers. A Model-T bus served as the first airport limousine.

In the middle of the field was a 208-foot high mooring mast for dirigibles. Ford wanted the lighter-than-aircraft, rigid airships to use his facility as well as the airplane. The Navy's pride of the skies, the dirigible *"Los Angeles,"* was a welcome visitor and attracted thousands.

This model airport was also the site for a specialized pilot training school Ford owned and operated. "Purchasers of planes are welcome to send their own men to our school for special training, if they meet the

Henry Ford had this special all-aluminum Model-T truck built to haul mail for Ford Air Transport Service. (Ford Archives Photo)

requirements," said a company announcement. "But we must ask them to consider our decision of their fitness final. So important do we regard this provision, that we reserve the right to decline to deliver a Ford plane unless the pilot who will fly it meets with the approval of the officials of our training school."

Such was the Air World of Henry Ford in the pre-Lindbergh era when most people thought the airplane was relegated to the cow pasture and the carnival air show.

Beyond all of this, Henry Ford knew there was something else needed to bring the full import of aviation before the public. Perhaps, he remembered how difficult it was to sell the public on the "horseless carriage" at the turn of the century. With the airplane, it would be much harder, he believed, because of the environment where the machine operated, the ocean of air above the earth. He set about to stimulate interest in aviation in a unique manner. The Ford Motor Company established the Edsel Ford Trophy for a commercial airplane reliability tour, patterned after the famous Glidden Tours in the early days of the automobile. An annual affair, The Ford Reliability Air Tour, it was said, meant more to the development of safety and efficiency for U.S. commercial aircraft than any other event.

Under terms laid down by Ford, only bona fide aircraft manufacturers could compete. Planes entered had to have a speed greater than 80-mph. All planes were required to carry, in addition to the pilot,

This was Edsel Ford Trophy awarded to winners of the Ford Reliability Air Tours of the late '20s and early '30s. Winners had their names engraved on special trophy plaque. Note symbols on globe showing all forms of transportation except sea-going vessels. Plane at top is 2-AT Ford "Air Transport."
(Ford Archives Photo)

The start of the first Ford Reliability Air Tour in 1925. There were seventeen planes of different makes entered in the inaugural event. *(Ford Archives Photo)*

The Ford "Flying Flivver" which Henry Ford had in mind to make the Model-T of aviation. Insert shows Lindbergh in cockpit. The famous flyer flew the plane when he visited Ford shortly after his famous Trans-Atlantic flight.

(Ford Archives Photo)

a payload of 0.5 pounds per cubic inch of their engine displacement. This payload could consist of passengers or ballast. The course these planes had to fly covered nearly 1900 miles, and was divided into 10-legs — Detroit to Fort Wayne to Chicago, to Omaha via Iowa City, to St. Joseph to Kansas City to St. Louis to Indianapolis to Columbus to Cleveland to Detroit.

There were seventeen entries on the starting line at Ford Airport for the first round-robin air junket on September 28, 1925. Just about every known make of plane was represented — three *Travelairs*, one *Waco*, one *Swallow*, one *Fokker*, one Curtiss *Carrier Pigeon*, two *Martins*, one Ford *Trimotor* and one *Yackey Sport* — biplanes and monoplanes, the best of their day. At their controls were some of the most famous pilots and flying sportsmen in the nation.

On October 4, of the original starters, fifteen returned to the starting point. Eleven had achieved a perfect score, and since there was no contest for leadership — reliability was the yardstick — all participants finishing on schedule were considered winners. Their names were engraved on the Edsel Ford Trophy. But more important, the Tour was a showcase for the planes of the day.

Every city visited welcomed the pilots with enthusiasm. Large crowds were attracted to the flying fields where the entries were scheduled to stop. Interest in aviation boomed.

The Tour continued under Ford sponsorship for several years and did much to promote the airplane. Meanwhile, Henry Ford was bent on getting into the private plane business as well as the commercial aviation field.

One day in 1926, he called newspapermen to the plant and made a little speech. "Aviation is bigger in possibilities than anything else in the world," he began. "It is too big to be a one-man patent concern; too big to be any one man's contribution to science."

Then, he cut his speech short and said — "Come on, I want to show you something."

Whereupon he took reporters into one part of the factory where big canvas cur-

Wreckage of Ford "Flying Flivver" which crashed during tests in Florida. Killed in the crash was Harry Brooks, Ford test pilot and close friend of Henry Ford. After crash Ford said he wanted to get out of aviation and he did for a long time. (Ford Archives Photo)

tains secreted the work going on. "Behind that curtain, gentlemen, is the Ford *Flying Flivver,*" Ford announced. "That's all. Now make up any kind of a story you want."

He turned and walked away. But he never did take them behind the curtain. The first time reporters knew what he really had been talking about, they saw a small, low-wing airplane flying at low altitude over the Detroit River and racing against one of Gar Wood's speedboats. Somebody casually remarked — "There goes Old Henry's Model-T of the air."

Ford built two of the small planes. They were single-place jobs, low-wing, powered with a two-cylinder, 36-horsepower engine. They had a cruising speed of about 100-mph, and weighed about 370 pounds. He never did anything to develop the model, although it might well have been a successful light sportplane.

There was little question, however, that he probably intended to one day build a cheap, lightplane that would give everyone a pair of wings. Whatever his plans, a tragic accident cut them short and took Ford out of aviation. One of his close friends, Harry Brooks, was killed during flight tests with the Flivver plane.

When Henry Ford heard about it, he gave orders to shut down the factory. Production of Ford-built trimotors was phased out in 1933. The test flight of a 5-AT model on June 7 that year marked the end of an era.

The next time an airplane of any kind had the Ford name connected with it was when the Air Corps, in 1940, started talking with the Ford people about mass producing a pursuit plane to help in the 50,000 plane program that President Roosevelt wanted. Henry Ford made the headlines again when he said he could mass produce planes like he built motor cars.

Ford originally discussed mass production of the Curtiss P-40 pursuit plane with Army Air Corps production people at Wright Field. But he never went ahead with this program. He first got into the aircraft program for World War II producing engines (Pratt & Whitney Wasps). Then, he built the largest under-one-roof factory in the world at Willow Run. There, he began producing the four-engined B-24 "Liberator" bombers. At peak production the Willow Run plant was turning out a plane an hour — a production figure he had predicted he could meet.

Major Ruben Fleet, then president of Consolidated Aircraft Corporation, designers of the B-24, summed up Henry Ford's role in the program: "He took the bomber, a complicated and what we thought was a hand-made and hand-tailored job at the time we built it, and with typical Ford mass production genius, put it on the Model V-8 assembly line."

In a far different way from which he ever dreamed, Henry Ford helped to put an end to the costliest war the world ever had suffered. The *Liberators* helped knock out Hitler's war-making potential in spectacular raids.

But it was not the four-engined bombers built at Willow Run that wrote the name Henry Ford indelibly into the pages of aviation history. His entry into the aircraft manufacturing field in 1924, his money and his ideas, launched the Air Age in the right direction with dedicated vision, purpose and mission.

The Ford Trimotor was the launch vehicle.

Ford put the 4-AT into mass production in 1926, and shown here is a part of the fuselage assembly line. Trimotor's skin was an alclad sandwich construction, aluminum on the outside as a rust preventative and duralumin on the inside for strength. Corrugated surface earned planes name of "Flying Washboards." *(Ford Archives Photo)*

CHAPTER THREE

Those Fabulous Flying Fords

WHEN the first of the 4-AT series production model Ford trimotors made their appearance in July of 1926, they caused quite a stir in the aviation community. The FORD emblem on the vertical fin in the tail, unquestionably, enhanced their acceptance, but the planes, themselves, caused many a lifted eyebrow, and generated a new feeling of public confidence in flying.

Perhaps, the three-engines had something to do with it. The trimotor concept, to many people, seemed a built-in safety factor. Indeed, it was. The Ford was designed to fly on two engines as well as it did on three; it could maintain level flight with only one engine operating. That, alone, spelled S-A-F-E-T-Y.

Then, there was the all-metal construction. Even to the layman and casual observer, the plane looked strong, tough and rugged, not put together with wire and cloth and wood and glue, like other aircraft of the period. Moreover, this all-metal characteristic was highly publicized. Ford saw to it the press informed the public about the metal construction.

The trimotor's skin was a sheet metal sandwich. The "bread" was thin slices of pure aluminum with high rust-resistant properties. The "meat" was duralumin, which had the sinews of steel. Adding to the strength, the skin was corrugated, which earned the planes another nickname — "the flying washboards."

By comparison with other planes and their cloth or veneer covered wings and fuselages, the Ford looked like a metallic giant. She was big, a fuselage length of 49 feet 10 inches, and a wing span of 74 feet, tip to tip. Gone were all struts and wires. Her thick wing, employing the cantilever, internally-braced construction, looked like it would lift anything. And strong enough to drive a Ford truck over it, which some claim they did to test its strength.

She had a fuselage outline of a cumbersome whale with a barn-door-like tail fin to steer her. But with her massive metal wing, she resembled a giant condor. Resting on her two main wheels and tail wheel when she taxied over the ground, she waddled like a gander. Probably why pilots dubbed her, affectionately, "The Tin Goose."

Before long, "the cry of the tin geese" would be heard in the skies from one end of the earth to the other.

The Wright J-6 engines, developing a 235-horsepower each, gave the 4-AT the look of power. Her rugged all-metal construction spelled strength, and the enormous wing said she was born to fly.   (Island Airlines Photo)

The cry was the throaty roar of her three engines. She had power — three air-cooled, radial, Wright J-6 engines each developing

The Model 4-AT trimotor had wicker-type chairs in cabin. Curtains hung at the windows and each passenger had individual light fixture. (Trans World Airlines Photo)

In later models, wicker-type chairs were replaced with more comfortable upholstered leather and fabric seats. Passenger in back in this picture is famed aviatrix Amelia Earhart. She helped pioneer first air-rail service in TAT Ford trimotor. (Trans World Airlines Photo)

approximately 225-horsepower. She had two-bladed, metal propellers. These powerplants gave her a cruising speed of close to 100-mph and a maximum speed of 130-mph, faster for her day than any other form of transportation.

Empty, she weighed about 6,500 pounds, but she had a gross weight of more than 10,000 pounds, and she could carry a payload of a ton or more. She could climb at the rate of 900 feet per minute to a maximum altitude of more than three miles, high enough to clear the highest mountain passes.

She was built for passenger comfort. There was over 400 cubic feet of cabin space, the passenger compartment being 16 feet long, six feet in height, more than four feet in width. There was room for 12-passengers, two rows of seats, six in a row on each side of a narrow aisle. She had big, half-moon picture windows on each side of the fuselage, and the location of her wing gave passengers a bird's-eye view that would be sorrowfully missed in the low-wing planes, destined to replace her on the airlanes.

For its day, the Ford trimotor cabin was luxury aloft. Seats were wicker-type chairs with leather cushions. Walls were highly-polished plywood paneling with decorative murals. Curtains hung from the windows. She was, perhaps, the true "Air Pullman" that Bill Stout had in mind.

From the passenger's standpoint, however, she had several faults. She was probably the noisiest plane ever built. She squealed and yowled. You had to cup your hands in the cockpit and shout to be heard. Back in the cabin it was almost as bad. They gave you cotton to stuff in your ears. She vibrated until your teeth ached. Mostly it was the control cables which were outside, and slapped against the fuselage. And she was cold as a flying ice box. There were no heaters in the early models.

But it really didn't matter, she was safe and strong, and she performed whatever task she was called upon to do, and did it well.

Up front, in the enclosed cockpit were two bucket seats, side-by-side, for pilot and co-pilot. One man could fly her without any stress or strain, but the idea of having two pilots and two sets of controls was another Ford approach to making the public "safety conscious." There was a minimum of instruments to worry about. The dashboard was almost too simple. And the controls! She had wooden-spoked steering wheels on the upright columns. These wheels came off the deluxe Model-T

Instrumentation on the Ford Trimotor consisted of an altimeter, rate of climb indicator, turn and bank indicator, airspeed indicator, magnetic compass, gyroscope and clock. The engine group included: Fuel gauges, tachometer, oil pressure and oil temperatures gauges, engine primers and inertia starters. The flight controls were dual and consisted of large auto-type steering wheels for actuating the elevators and ailerons, with stirrups for rudder control. The hydraulic wheel brakes were operated by a single gearshift-type lever located between seats.
(Trans World Airlines Photo)

automobile. You pushed forward or backward to move the elevators up or down; turned the wheel, right or left, to wiggle the ailerons. Wide, brake-like pedals moved the rudder. But a standard gearshift in the center, operated the brakes. On the ground, taxiing, you steered with the engines. Small, knob-topped levers in a cluster of three, mounted in the center and below the dash, gave a pilot a fistful of horsepower. She had self-starters, switches off the "Tin Lizzy's" dash, one for each engine. Trim control was a small crank above and behind the pilot.

They used to say — "Ford pilots are circus freaks. They all grow three hands after the first 100 hours."

But pilots loved the "Tin Goose." The high-lift wing hiked her off the ground in a hurry. She could become airborne in three plane lengths. They said she was like America's pioneer women on the wagon trains — hard-working and strong, not much for frills, but always feminine, understanding, forgiving and obedient. The Ford had excellent control responses. There was no question she was a flying machine! Whatever took place was an honest marriage between the pilot and the airplane.

Mechanics liked her, too. There was easy access to her engines when they needed repairs. Her skin seldom needed any patches. Gas tanks in the "Turtle Back" (capacity 271 gallons) simplified fueling operations. They could wash her down with a hose.

Such was the plane that Henry Ford built and put on the market more than forty

The first Ford 4-AT trimotor was put into service on the Ford-owned airline. Here, the plane is being loaded with Model-T parts for shipment to Chicago plant. *(Ford Archives Photo)*

Sometimes interiors of Ford Air Transport Service planes were stripped down for freight. On this flight complete Model-T was flown from Detroit to Cleveland.
(Ford Archives Photo)

years ago. Even the price tag was attractive — $42,000, fully-equipped and ready to fly. F.O.B. Detroit, bright and shiny on the ramp at the most modern airport in the U. S. Tanks filled with gas, for good customer relationship.

II

THE first customer? Guess who? Why, The Ford Motor Company of Dearborn, Michigan, naturally. And almost immediately the first 4-AT license Number NC-1492 was put into service on the company-operated Detroit-Chicago airline. The second plane, NC-4309 went to National Air Transport (NAT) a forerunner of United Air Lines, which was flying the mail over the "Hell Stretch" of the Alleghenies, New York to Chicago. Plane No. 3 was sold to the U. S. Navy designated XJR-1, to be

Wealthy sportsmen were among first private purchasers of the flying Fords. This was the interior of New York millionaire's plane. Henry Ford, ironically, never owned one for personal use although at the time he was world's only billionaire! (Ford Archives Photo)

U.S. Navy was third customer to buy one of the Ford trimotors. This is Navy version (XJR-1) in front of dirigible hangar at Lakehurst, New Jersey Naval Air Station.
(Ford Archives Photo)

Army Air Corps cargo version, designated C-9, was used for personnel transport and freight operations, the beginning of the first air transport squadrons and military airlift.
(Ford Archives Photo)

Standard Oil Company was first private corporation to purchase one of the Ford 4-AT planes. Many other companies followed suit, using the big planes as executive ships, the beginning of the present day corporate aircraft fleets. (Ford Archives Photo)

used as a personnel transport and for submarine patrol.

By the time fifteen 4-ATs had rolled off the line, they proudly wore the colors and insignia of Stout Air Services, The Standard Oil Company, Royal Typewriter Company, Maddux Airlines and the U. S. Army Air Corps (the XC-9) a cargo transport. Another, plane No. 11, went to Marcell N. Rand of New York City, the first Ford trimotor sold to a private individual. Significantly, the design was not yet a year old, before Ford had penetrated every segment of aviation — the air transport industry, business or corporate flying, and the private plane market.

Meanwhile, something happened that swept the nation like a tidal wave of enthusiasm to give aviation a booster shot in the arm. An unknown air mail pilot, Michigan-born, Charles A. Lindbergh, startled the world and changed it, when he flew his "Spirit of St. Louis" monoplane non-stop, New York to Paris. The effect was electrifying; everybody wanted a slice of the "pie in the sky." Small airline operators popped up like mushrooms all over the country.

Henry Ford, although he was interested in promoting air transportation and predicted a great future for it, did not like to fly. In summer of 1927, shortly after his return from Paris following his historic Atlantic solo crossing, Lindbergh visited Dearborn Airport and took Ford up for his first and last airplane ride. Shown here, helmeted Lindbergh helps Ford into trimotor. At left is William B. Mayo, nominal Chief Engineer Ford Motor Company who was placed in charge of Airplane Division. Bill Stout stands directly behind Lindbergh and at far right is Edsel Ford. (Ford Archives Photo)

The Ford Trimotor was the answer to many of their problems.

Bill Stout started his own Stout Air Lines Company in 1927 operating between Grand Rapids, and Detroit, Michigan. The author remembers it well. My second airplane ride was aboard one of Stout's airliners. We made the trip in little more than an hour from Grand Rapids to the Ford Airport. Returning, it took us more than four hours — in a Model-T Ford. A good example of the speed of air transport against ground transport.

Stout's airline was important because it carried only passengers. There was no revenue from mail pay. In this respect, Stout was a daring operator, pioneering again. The line never made any profit. Planes seldom carried more than three or four passengers, and Stout abandoned the operation. But bigger operators watched it closely and, unquestionably, it stimulated interest in all-passenger air services. Stout Air Service was of the first generation in a whole new family of air transportation.

Jack Maddux, a Los Angeles car dealer, was another pioneer. He started Maddux Airlines, flying between Los Angeles and San Francisco. He bought Ford Trimotor No. 7 but there was a stipulation. The plane had to prove it could fly over the hump-back of the treacherous Rockies.

Another Ford test pilot, Larry Fritz, accepted the challenge and in June of 1927, a month after Lindbergh's epoch flight, he flew the plane from Dearborn to L.A. Maddux was so pleased, he promptly ordered a second plane, and before the 4-AT series was discontinued Maddux Airlines operated a fleet of five Fords.

Scenic Airways of Grand Canyon, Arizona (it later became Grand Canyon Airlines) bought Plane No. 22, and its unique operation exemplified the Ford's wide-range of performance capabilities. Grand Canyon Airlines flew its plane on a 160-mile run

The author flew in this early Stout Air Lines trimotor from Grand Rapids to Detroit over forty years ago! There was a "flight escort" on board, and passengers were served hot coffee and sandwiches — air travel deluxe, vintage 1928.
(Ford Archives Photo)

Probably the most famous Ford trimotor is "The Floyd Bennett" (above) which Bernt Balchen flew over the South Pole with Comdr. Richard E. Byrd and party, November 28-29 in 1929. Plane was named after Floyd Bennett, who had flown Byrd over North Pole in 1926.   *(Ford Archives Photo)*

After flight over South Pole "The Floyd Bennett" (below) was buried in snow at Little America. Some 20 years later, Byrd returned with another expedition and they dug the plane out, warmed it up, and flew it. The plane today rests in Ford Museum at Greenfield Village, Dearborn, Michigan. (Ford Archives Photo)

through . . . not over . . . the big gorge. It was routine to drop down into the rock cut — 3,000 feet below the canyon rim — and away they went. Ferrying sight-seers, shuttling passengers between Canyon City and Lake Mead (Hoover Dam), toting supplies to isolated ranchers, operating from "air strips" not much longer than a football field.

"We scared the daylights out of passengers," recalled Ed Campbell, who flew for GCA. "We'd drop through the clouds and fly down a tunnel between cloud cover, river, and canyon walls. It was spooky, but safe enough. The Ford was a very forgiving airplane. She could get you out of almost anything you could get her into."

On the Grand Canyon route the Fords served science. They conducted the first aerial investigation of the great gorge, contributing much to man's knowledge of the biggest hole on earth.

Plane No. 15 played another scientific role. Christened *"The Floyd Bennett,"* after the famous polar flyer who flew Byrd over the North Pole (May 9, 1926 in *"The Josephine Ford"*), the plane took off from the first "Little America" on Thanksgiving Day, 1929, with Byrd and four others aboard. They were headed for the South Pole.

The plane was a stock 4-AT model equipped with skis and heavy duty engine. The ship sagged under an appalling overload. But at 3:15 P.M. she was airborne. Then, picking up a tail wind, she droned south over the desolate Ross Barrier.

Mountains barricading the Antarctic ice cap constituted the main obstacle. Hopefully, *"The Floyd Bennett"* could lift her six-ton gross weight 10,000 feet, clearing the saddle at the head of Liv's Glacier. At 8:15 P.M. Byrd dropped photographic plates to a geological party sledging near the Queen Maud Mountains. Then he swung south, to do combat with the Liv hump.

Slowly, the "Tin Goose" waddled up the glacier, climbing to 8,000 feet. The pass loomed above, with grim rock battlements closing in on both sides. There was no room to turn around.

Pilot Bernt Balchen shouted back that they had to lighten the ship: "Two hundred pounds! Or we'll never make it!"

Byrd frowned. Should it be gas, or food? The fuel margin was painfully low: but there were scant rations for the trek home if they crashed. They dumped a 125-pound bag of precious foodstuffs. The plane's performance improved, but downdrafts coming over Mt. Nansen pressed the Ford closer and closer to the ice.

Balchen yelled, "We're stalling! Dump out some more!"

Byrd nodded, and another sack of food went out the door, a month's supply of precious rations . . . minutes ticked by, the *"The Floyd Bennett"* shivered and vibrated, throttles at the fire-wall. With seconds to spare, she clawed up an extra 300 feet, mushed over the saddle, and swept out onto the vast glacier plateau . . .

At 1:15 a.m. Byrd, who was navigating, told Balchen to circle. He shot a fix. "Ninety, South!" Byrd shouted.

They were over the pole.

The Norwegian explorer, Roald Amundsen, who was first to reach the South Pole by sled (December 17, 1911) had taken five months to make the trip. *"The Floyd Bennett"* made the round-trip in 20 hours. Never again would men foot-slog in the desolate Antarctic; the "Tin Goose" had found a better way.

Of all the Ford trimotors built, *"The Floyd Bennett"* probably is the most famous. No Ford ever flew the Atlantic or the Pacific.

The reason why the Ford Trimotors weren't popular among the record-smashers, the globe-girdlers and ocean-hoppers, perhaps, is because they were too busy pioneering air transportation. The small family of airlines using Fords, grew and grew and grew. And as the bigger airline companies emerged, the demand was for bigger payloads, more airplane.

Ford had the answer in the 5-AT model, the same basic design, but a larger airplane. The 5-AT-1 (NX-6926) was bought by Pratt & Whitney Aircraft Company of Hartford, Connecticut, a logical purchaser since the new plane was powered with P&W engines. The powerful trio of WASP engines, built by Pratt & Whitney, developed a total of more than 1200-horsepower, which permitted a larger airframe, and provided improved performance.

Production line in new factory showing larger 5-AT models in final assembly. This plane, a 5-AT-D was equipped with NACA ring cowlings on outboard engines, a version preferred by some airlines because of slightly increased speed. (Ford Archives Photo)

The 5-AT model had a wing span four feet longer than the 4-AT and was about two feet greater in fuselage length. But increased cabin space permitted carrying 13 to 15 passengers, appealing to the airline operators. Even more important were improved performance figures.

The larger trimotor could carry a payload of 3800 pounds almost double that of the 4-AT. She was five to ten miles per hour faster, but operating costs remained proportionately the same. The 5-AT model sold for $55,000. The market was almost ready-made.

By the time the big trimotors were in production, the air transport industry was beginning to evolve into something more than a hodge-podge of independents and fly-by-night operators. Businessmen, stimulated to invest in aviation's future by Lindbergh's flight and amendments to the Air Mail Act incorporating a profit motive, got into airline management. There arose a healthier family of air carriers. Names like Eastern Air Transport, American Airways, Northwest Airways, Transcontinental Air Transport, Pan American Airways, began to appear on time-tables — forerunners all of today's major trunklines that comprise the Jet Age Scheduled Air Transport Industry. In most cases, the Ford trimotors figured in their early operations.

An important milestone in passenger operations was the advent of Transcontinental Air Transport (TAT) which inaugurated a unique air/rail, coast-to-coast service. TAT bought six of the first dozen 5-AT's to start the operation.

The scene was New York's big Pennsylvania Railroad station on July 4, 1929 where passengers boarded Pullman railcars for the first leg of the journey, New York to Columbus, Ohio. (Flying over the Allegheny Mountains at night was considered too much of a risk.) But next morning at Columbus, the Ford trimotor was waiting.

New York City Police Commissioner Grover Whalen, left, was among those on hand as Amelia Earhart, then assistant to the traffic manager of TAT, christened the Ford tri-motor "City of New York" at ceremonies in Pennsylvania Station July 7, 1929, inaugurating TAT's new coast-to-coast air-rail service. Col. Lindbergh piloted the "City of Los Angeles" only as far as Winslow, Ariz., on the eastbound inaugural flight. On July 9 he piloted the first westbound plane into the Los Angeles terminal.   (TWA/Acme Photo)

The TAT air/rail service was abandoned, but shortly afterwards the airline started flying Ford trimotors at night as well as by day, the beginning of coast-to-coast all passenger, scheduled air service. This is TAT's "City of Columbus," first plane to make the westbound trip. The Ford's performance permitted it to fly over highest mountains. (Trans World Airlines Photo)

Passengers transferred from train to plane at a special station built at the edge of the airport. On the first air-leg, flying entirely in daylight hours, the Fords whisked the aerial voyagers westward to Waynoka, Oklahoma. There, at the airport, specially designed, tear-drop "aero-cars" took passengers to the Sante Fe Depot, where they boarded another Pullman for the overnight ride to Clovis, New Mexico. At Clovis, they boarded another Ford airliner for the flight to Los Angeles. The entire trip took about 48 hours which was faster than any other means, and remarkably reliable — but it really didn't save much more than half a day over straight rail travel.

The cost of a ticket (about 16 cents per mile) was so expensive that it attracted only a limited luxury class, and even the rich, in those pre-depression days, didn't fill up the planes. The experiment lost almost $3,000,000 in the first eighteen months (it was an all-passenger line, no mail pay) and the service was abandoned. But history must record that the Ford Trimotors had pioneered the first effort at transcontinental passenger air travel without benefit of mail subsidy.

Moreover, within eighteen months (after TAT had become Transcontinental & Western Air, Inc., the parent company of today's Trans World Airlines) the Ford trimotors started flying at night. You could cross the continent all the way by plane in about 36-hours. The "Tin Goose" had laid the golden egg that hatched into a bonanza, the golden age of air transport.

Tragedy over the plains of Kansas, focused attention on the Fords, and airlines the world over rushed to get in their orders for the all-metal trimotors. The tragedy was the death of famed Notre Dame football coach, Knute Rockne, killed in the crash of a Fokker trimotor, when the wing fell off during a thunderstorm. After that, the wooden planes were doomed. For a while, the Fords became the "old reliables and the indestructables" for airlines everywhere.

Foreign orders piled up, and the "Tin Geese" made the world their home. In Europe, Asia, Africa, Australia, Central and South America they were common sights at air terminals. It has been said that in a world and a period when just about everybody owned one, or had heard of the Ford Model-T automobiles, there were some isolated spots, where the name *Ford* was synonymous with "airplane."

Then, in the early thirties, came a revolution in aircraft design with the advent of the Boeing 247, twin-engined, low-wing, high-speed (200-mph) 10-passenger transport planes, and the Douglas DC-1, 12-passenger airliner. The cumbersome, slower Ford Trimotors simply couldn't keep up with the newcomers. One by one

When Kansas crash of Fokker trimotor killed famed coach Knute Rockne, TWA (Transcontinental & Western Air, Inc., forerunner of today's Trans World Airlines) turned to the all-metal Ford as the workhorse of its fleet. This was typical scene at Grand Central Air Terminal, Glendale, California the western terminus of the coast-to-coast airline. *(Trans World Airlines Photo)*

The advent of the Douglas DC-1, twelve-passenger, luxury transport which was much faster than the Fords, brought a new dimension to air travel. The scene at Glendale looked like this in the early thirties when TWA introduced the new Douglas on its routes. Later models, the DC-2 and DC-3 ended the reign of the Ford trimotor as "Queen" of the airlanes. *(Trans World Airlines Photo)*

Technological progress permitted changing the configuration of the Fords to achieve better performance. Plane at right shows efforts made to streamline the "Tin Goose" with engine cowlings and wheel pants.
(Ford Archives Photo)

the airlines phased them out of the picture. They said the planes that Ford built were destined for the same fate as the Model-T when the Model-A took the center of the stage.

It was not entirely the equipment evolution, or revolution, either, because Ford had already shut down the production line for the 4-AT and the 5-AT models *before* the first Boeing or the first Douglas had flown in airline service. Altogether there were 198 Ford Trimotors produced in one configuration or another (and two other experimental designs) in the seven years between 1926-33 that Henry Ford was in the airplane manufacturing business. Each in its own way contributed to the advancement of air transportation.

III

THERE were many different variations in powerplants, cabin interiors, streamlining and other features incorporated in the Ford trimotors built at the Dearborn factory. They put the famous NACA (National Advisory Committee For Aeronautics, today's NASA) ring cowlings around the engines to improve the airflow characteristics. In another approach to streamlining, they put "wheel pants" around the main wheels and "faired" the landing gear strut arrangement. They equipped the planes with king-sized pontoons to make them seaplanes, and then they put wheels on the floats to make them amphibians. They tried two-bladed props, three-bladed props and even four-bladed props in a variety of powerplant configurations. In one experimental version, they ironed out the washboard skin and covered the airframe with sleek, smooth, aluminum-duralumin alloy. It was like putting a tux on a tramp. They went back to the corrugated skin, a distinctive feature, symbol of the Ford's ruggedness. But no matter what they did, the basic airframe wasn't changed very

This Ford 5-AT model was fitted with pontoons each of which weighed more than the Ford "Flying Flivver." Float-equipped plane, pilots reported, handled as well as the landplane version. (Ford Archives Photo)

Another modification produced this awkward-looking, cumbersome Amphibian. (Ford Archives Photo)

One of early model 4-AT trimotors was sold to the Royal Typewriter Company and used in spectacular promotion stunt. Called the "Air Truck" the plane hauled typewriters aloft which were dropped by parachute over various cities. In group standing by plane, at right, is Bill Stout. (Ford Archives Photo)

much, and the Fords performed ambidextrously a multitude of tasks.

One such versatile craft was Plane No. 8, a 4-AT sold to the Royal Typewriter Company, converted into an Air Truck, capacity 210 Royal typewriters.

One of trimotors sold to Monarch Foods had this unusual interior. The "Flying Grocery Store" visited many cities in mid-west to promote new canned food products.
(Ford Archives Photo)

It had a special fuselage hatch (no windows) and the crew would drop the typewriters by parachute. Of course, it was all part of a promotion sales campaign — a Royal drop from the skies!

The special "Club" models of the 5-AT-C and 5-AT-D series were something else again. Elegant, super deluxe interiors, like Plane NC-432H sold to Marshall Chang Hsueh-Liang, Peiping, China. The price tag was upped by $15,000 for such luxurious interiors — soft, upholstered, swivel chairs, divans, dining-room table furnishings, special light fixtures, owner-selected cabin decor, paneling and even wallpaper with fancy designs!

There was also the "Flying Grocery Store," plane model 4-AT-B, NC-7863, which was owned by Monarch Foods. The stripped-down interior was lined with the various Monarch products. And for two years, 1929-31, this flying showcase flew all over the mid-west, visiting numerous cities, promoting the Monarch name on canned goods.

Many other promotional schemes employed the Ford trimotors, and in one form or another changed their configuration. Sometimes, they modified the planes for more practical purposes. Pan American-Grace Airways, for instance, cut a hatch

10-feet long in the top of a 5-AT fuselage, so it could load 740 pounds of heavy machinery. TWA, in one configuration put baggage bins in the wings.

In military versions (Navy and Marine RJ and later RDs) they were modified as cargo planes, flying ambulances, paratroop carriers. One Navy version became a Torpedo Bomber. The Army Air Corps bought thirteen altogether. Designated C-9 cargo transports, they became the nucleus of early Army air transport squadrons. The Army Air Corps even got a look at one Ford as a bomber.

They modified one 5-AT-C and entered it in a bomber design competition. Built very secretly, the bomber version, designated XB-906, had a modified single-place cockpit, a glass "greenhouse" in the bottom of the nose for the bombardier, internal bomb racks, and two open-cockpit positions for machine gunners. During tests in September, 1931, the XB-906 crashed, killing Ford test pilot LeRoy Manning.

Another Ford Trimotor few people ever heard about, was the Model 14-AT, a 40-passenger giant, Henry Ford's idea of the airliner of the future which, admittedly, was far ahead of its time. But it made its appearance (it never flew) in one of the worst times in the nation's history — February, 1932, mid-winter in the mid-depression years. Moreover, the better designed, faster planes were "on the drawing boards" at Boeing Airplane Company in Seattle and Douglas Aircraft Company in Santa Monica, California, their revolutionary approach to the airliner destined to make the 14-AT obsolete before she was rolled out onto the factory ramp at Ford Airport.

But the big Ford Transport was really something in her own right, with far-reaching impact. McGraw Hill's authoratative aeronautical publication *Aviation Magazine*, summed it up in the April, 1932 issue — *"The saying that engineering development progresses most rapidly in periods of business depression finds no better illustration than in the recent activities of the Ford Motor Company. With general business conditions at their lowest ebb in the industrial history of the country, Mr. Ford has seen fit to take advantage of the reduced pressure on his*

In one experimental version engines were located in the wings, similar to the idea Stout had used in his original 3-AT "Air Pullman" trimotor. Nothing came of the modification. In background, is replica of Independence Hall which Ford had built at Greenfield Village. It still stands. (Ford Archives Photo)

The trimotor that wasn't a trimotor! This experimental version, basically the airframe of the "Tin Goose" was powered with single Pratt & Whitney 1,000-horsepower engine fitted with latest NACA cowling and driving three-bladed propeller. It was used as aerial freighter. Note porthole windows. Only one was built.
(Ford Archives Photo)

This XB-906 bomber version of the 5-AT was entered in military competition at Dayton, Ohio in 1934. It crashed during series of tests.
(U.S. Army Air Corps Photo)

Henry Ford never stopped pioneering. In 1931, he built this giant "airliner of the future." Designated the 14-AT, the plane was far ahead of its era. The four-bladed propellers and engines "hidden" in the wings represented advanced thinking in aerodynamic design. Plane never flew. It was the last of the trimotors.
(Ford Archives Photo)

Front view of 14-AT shows unusual engine arrangement. Altogether the three engines produced 2540-horsepower, more than any other U.S.-built aircraft up to that time. It was also the only Ford trimotor using water-cooled, in-line engines.
(Ford Archives Photo)

production departments to engineer radical departures from established standards in both the automotive and aeronautical fields. The long expected eight-cylinder car, and a large passenger transport airplane involving features never before attempted in American design practice, are the tangible results of these efforts."

The 14-AT was a monster, 110-feet from wing tip to wing tip, a fuselage length of over 80-feet, nose to tail. A radical departure in design was the engine arrangement. She had two 720-horsepower, water-cooled Hispano engines literally "hidden" inside the thick wing, an extreme approach to streamlining practices. These outboard engines drove four-bladed wooden propellers. The third engine, an 1100-horsepower "W"-type Hispano-Suiza was mounted in a highly streamlined nacelle over the center section of the wing, driving a three-bladed, Hamilton-Standard steel-alloy propeller. The combined 2600-horsepower was more horses than any other aircraft to date.

More significant, however, were the visionary cabin accommodations and configuration. Immediately in back of the pilots' compartment which had big square windows, ideal visibility, and room enough to almost call it a "flight deck," was a smoking room, even though Ford abhorred the habit. Continuing aft along a center aisle, there were two passenger compartments, two washrooms (one on each side) followed by two more passenger compartments. Each of the four main passenger compartments had seating accommodations for eight persons.

Except for the very narrow center aisle, each of these compartments were the same dimension as a double-section in the standard railway Pullman car. The seats were Pullman-width and they could be converted into berths.

There was a galley equipped with a stove and refrigerator. In-flight meal service was lurking there, too, in the mind of the genius. He had already started the idea of the "Flight Escort" aboard the Ford Air Transport Service planes. A built-in "announciator" system permitted passengers to summon the steward from any compartment. The cabin was also insulated for sound, walls and ceiling being of double construction throughout, enclosing a relatively large volume of dead air space. A complete thermostat-controlled heating and ventilating system provided living room comfort for the passengers.

This was the Ford model 14-AT, the plane of tomorrow, born yesterday, doomed to die before she spread her wings.

Probably what influenced most the decision to not even fly the plane was the appearance of the twin-engined Boeing 10-passenger Model 247 and the Douglas DC-2, 14-passenger airliners. With their near 200-mile-an-hour speeds, the big Ford Transport could never keep up, and the axiom in air transport was and still is — "We're selling SPEED. Without it, you may as well take the train."

When the Boeings (in 1933) and the Douglas DC-2 (in 1934) began flying regular scheduled operation, one by one the airlines turned their backs on the Ford Trimotors. Progress had caught up with progress, and the faithful "Tin Geese" were doomed, just as they, in turn, had spelled *finis* for the veneer-covered Fokker trimotors. Within five years, almost all of the Fords had disappeared from the major trunklines, and in the late thirties the DC-2 and an improved plane, the 21-passenger Douglas DC-3, were carrying 95 per cent of all the world's air commerce.

But, where, oh where, did the "Tin Goose" go?

IV

IT has been roughly estimated (from military and Federal Aviation Agency sources) that approximately two-thirds of all the Ford Trimotors built were either victims of crashes or scrapped. During their ten year reign in the air, carrying the load for the airlines all over the world, the planes were overworked. There was a good share of crashes, but in no instance, did investigators prove structural failure. The all-metal construction paid off handsomely. It must be remembered, too, that when she was "queen of the airlanes" the airways, themselves, were a far cry from the modern system we have today. Fords helped pioneer night flying, airborne communications and many navigational aids. Until the late

Before the Boeing 247 and the Douglas DC-1, DC-2 and DC-3 airliners replaced them, the Ford trimotors were the most popular planes with early air travelers. Here is part of the airline fleet in the early thirties when the "Tin Goose" was the pride of the airways. (Ford Archives Photo)

thirties the safety of flying, despite all the Fords did to improve it, was still considered marginal. Bad weather and pilot error took a heavy toll.

Despite the plague of "crash fever", what hurt worst of all, however, was that the airlines abandoned her, courting the new skyships. Even so, they did so reluctantly and with tearful, nostalgic feeling. A TWA announcement in 1934 when the airline replaced its fleet of Fords with DC-2's read — *"Like faithful old fire-horses, unshod and retired to a life of ease and green pastures, a fleet of veteran trimotored airplanes is facing retirement after almost a decade of active service on the mid-transcontinental airway between New York and Los Angeles."*

John Collings, one-time Ford test pilot and later a TWA executive would write — "The end is in sight for the old girl. She was and is a thoroughbred, but her days are almost up."

How wrong he was. When U. S. airlines wrote her off, the "Tin Goose" migrated to other regions. They had written her obituary, but like Tom Sawyer she came back to attend her own funeral.

Who said the "Tin Goose" was dead?

Lowell Yerex, pioneer airline operator in Central America gathered together a flock of 5-AT's as fast as he could get them, and put them in service for TACA (*Transportes Aereos Centro-Americanos*) covering most of the countries south of the border. For the most part TACA's planes served as aerial freighters, including one "flying tanker" modified to carry 600 gallons of diesel fuel oil. It flew 2400 gallons a day to one mining operation.

Another fleet of Fords turned up in South America, shuttling supplies to mine operations over the Andes Mountains. They were also pressed into service in Alaska and the jungles of New Guinea. Others operated in Mexico, Guatemala, and Australia where the R.A.A.F. (Royal Australian Air Force) made one an ambulance plane.

At home, in the U. S., Fords still roamed the skies although they were virtually extinct from airline operations. But in the late thirties they were in great demand by a second generation of "Barnstormers". The breed popped up at county fairs and carnivals. The trimotor could land in virtually any cow pasture or fairgrounds area, and at a nominal fee per head (capacity 15 passengers) for a ten minute ride, it was like money in the bank for the gypsy flyer. At least, one trimotor found herself a star performer at the National Air Races.

Harold Johnson, stunt flyer, put on the act — looping the Ford at low level in front of the grandstand. It was a thrill to watch, as the author did, at the Cleveland Air Races in 1939 when Johnson stunted the plane for the last time.

A hundred thousand pairs of eyes watched the glistening, silvery Ford take off and circle the field. Then, swooping down out of the sky she came *flying upside down*, doughnut tires on big struts reaching skyward, the tip of the rudder almost scraping sparks on the concrete runway. Then, Johnson pulled her up... up... into a chandelle. After that he did slow rolls, snap rolls and Immelmans, acrobatics reserved for fighter planes, but she performed like an aerialist on the circus trapeze. The show climaxed with loop-the-loop! More than a thrilling spectacle, it proved that the Ford was probably the toughest, most rugged plane ever built.

The outbreak of World War II in Europe in 1939, cancelled out the National Air Races for a time, and the stunting Ford disappeared from the scene. But the "Tin Goose" found herself a role in the air war during the early stages of the conflict.

We find her operating as a transport with the famous Flying Tigers in China, *before* Pearl Harbor. Another Ford trimotor, an Army C-9 transport, turned up in the Phillippines and was used to evacuate civilians from Bataan. Back and forth she shuttled refugees between Bataan and Corregidor, until the Japs got too close and shot her wings off while she was taking on another load of evacuees on the Rock.

General George C. Kenney, MacArthur's Air Chief in the South Pacific, recalls that a couple of Fords were used as transports when his Fifth Air Force had very little else in the form of flyable equipment.

In Europe, after Italy's surrender, an eye witness account says some Ford trimotors were used by Italian Air Force pilots, now with the Allies, for dropping ammunition and other supplies to the underground in Yugoslavia. The old Fords operated from a field near Toronto, Italy and flew at night to perform their mission.

The war over, with big, four-engined transport planes in the skies, and everybody waiting for the age of air travel to explode into a real bonanza, attention was suddenly focused on a unique airline operation back at home. Island Airways, based in Port Clinton, Ohio in 1946 was flying a fleet of Ford trimotors from the mainland to a small group of islands in Lake Erie.

Paradoxically, the "Tin Goose" had found herself a new home and a new life within a radius of 100 miles from the old Ford Airport at Dearborn, Michigan where she had been born 20 years before.

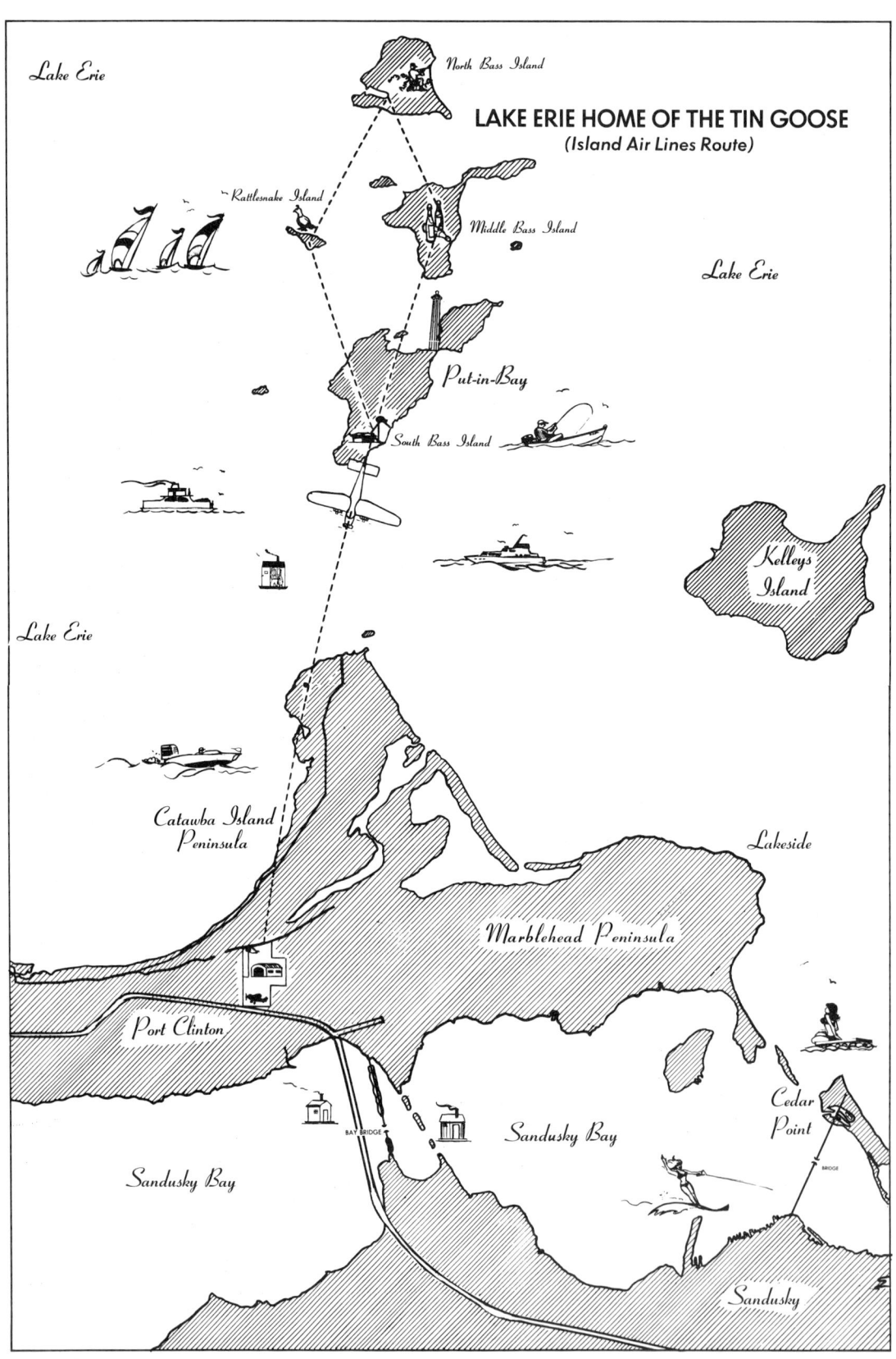

CHAPTER FOUR

Island Home Of The "Tin Goose"

ABOUT two hours before, I was sipping champagne and savoring a luncheon steak five miles above the earth in the quiet, spacious cabin on a 600-mile-an-hour Boeing 727 jetliner. There was stereo music, mini-skirted hostesses waiting on us, and the temperature-controlled atmosphere offered living room comfort. All the luxuries of modern air travel.

What a contrast! Now, I am flying in another airliner, a thick-winged, Ford trimotor, the famous "Tin Goose", lumbering along at eighty miles an hour, about five hundred feet above ice-covered Lake Erie.

It is mid-January, 1968.

This machine in which I am flying was built in 1928 — forty years ago — the oldest of her breed still in daily operation.

No, we aren't on any special flight, an airline's publicity stunt. There are twelve other passengers back in the cabin, half a dozen sacks of U. S. mail, two lop-eared, yapping, hound dogs, a power snow-blower, and a variety of other miscellaneous cargo jammed in wherever there is space. This is a regular, scheduled trip on Island Airlines, which flies an average of five round-trips a day from its home base in Port Clinton, Ohio to the small group of islands just off shore in Lake Erie about half-way between Toledo and Cleveland.

Because of the full load, Ralph Dietrick, the pilot, lets me ride up front in the right-hand seat. There, in the cramped cockpit with no sound-proofing, and only a few feet away from the three big Wright J67-235-horsepower radials, the roar is deafening. The control cables on the outside of the fuselage, slapping against the corrugated skin, sets up vibrations that make your teeth ache. It is shivering cold; no heaters, just raw airplane.

Island Airlines' home base at Port Clinton, Ohio. "The Shortest Airline In The World" flies daily schedules between the mainland and a small group of islands just off shore in Lake Erie. (Island Airlines Photo)

With Ralph Dietrick at the controls, the oldest flying Ford trimotor races with the "Golden Eagle" enroute to Promontory, Utah to commemorate the 100th anniversary of the joining of the Union Pacific and Central Pacific railroads — the first transcontinental line. This "Tin Goose" will be 50 years old in 1978.
(Photo credit to Ron Ziel and Island Airlines)

True "Island Home of the Tin Goose" is this airport at Put-In-Bay (South Bass Island) where Island Airlines has hangars, restaurant and SKYTEL. Runway is about 1500 feet long, but Fords can get off the ground in 200 feet, are ideal for short-haul, short-field operations. (Island Airlines Photo)

And there is the smell of fish! The annual Erie "Perch Derby" is in full-swing. "Isaac Waltons" are here from everywhere, to try their luck. The fishing is good, Ralph tells me, and almost every returning angler boards with a gunnysack full of the tasty yellow-bellies. The airline business is so good they don't have time to get the fish smell out.

Who cares? This is *really* flying! An unforgettable, nostalgic trip into aviation's yesteryear. Air travel (except for the fish odor) as it was in the roaring 20's, when the "Tin Goose" helped start most of the fledgling airlines in this country.

It is a bright, clear day with plenty of blue sky, little or no wind, perfect for flying. Below, and dead ahead looms the largest of the islands, South Bass, about an eight minute flight from the mainland. Put-in-Bay is the name of the village, a small resort community, rich in American history. There, Commodore Oliver Hazard Perry's victorious fleet "put-in-bay" after defeating the British in the War of 1812. Every school child remembers Perry's famous message — *"We have met the enemy and they are ours!"* The naval engagement was fought in this maritime arena. And today, a 352-foot-high Doric column, Perry's monument, stands as a National Park Service shrine to the British and American sailors who died in the great sea battle.

Obligingly, Ralph circles the monument so I can take a picture. Then, he levels off, and our "Tin Goose" wallows down out of the sky to land at Put-In-Bay Airport. This is really her "Island Home."

The airport has a paved runway. There are two hangars, and a long, two-story terminal building. On the main floor is a ticket office, recreation room and rest room facilities. But upstairs are modern motel units, Ralph's SKYTEL. Across the road is a small restaurant, and a swimming pool. All around the field's perimeter are camping sites and cottages. The Ford trimotors built all of this.

Since 1935, they have been the aerial link with the mainland although one can, if one desires, make the trip in ferry boats, the only way automobiles get on the big island. But in winter, when the ice comes, the ferries stop running. Only "The Tin Goose" still goes. In the distant past, big iron-clad boats were the only means of travel in winter until the flying Fords came.

Taking on passengers at Put-In-Bay Terminal. Island Airlines also operates small planes to accommodate charter flights to the outer islands. (Island Airlines Photo)

We are on the ground briefly at Put-in-Bay. Ralph only kills the starboard engine, the other two are still idling, to save time. Five passengers disembark, and two more get aboard. They load some freight, an outboard motor and some camping equipment. Then, we're off again.

This time we are heading for Middle Bass, less than three miles away. The Ford is airborne in about 400 feet, Monument high by the time the island shore is behind us. The wheels are still spinning when Ralph sets the plane down at Middle Bass, minutes later.

Here, we lose three more of our passengers. They are commuters. Two of them live on the mainland, but they work in the famous Lonz Winery on Middle Bass. The third is Rev. William E. Ferguson, Rector of the St. Paul's Episcopal Church at Put-in-Bay. He teaches school at Middle Bass, and flies to his classroom every day.

The good Reverend tells us that next year two of his students will be flying each day, morning and evening, to and from Middle Bass to attend Put-in-Bay High School. Island Airlines has flown as many as five school-children back and forth each day from the northern islands to their high school classrooms on South Bass. For the youngsters in this region, flying is a way of life from the day they are born. It is said, they are reared on "Tin Goose" rhymes, and the roar of the flying Fords is their lullaby.

Taking off from Middle Bass, our next stop is Rattlesnake Island, smallest of the inland lake's archipelago. Rattlesnake got its name, not because there are so many of this specie of serpent present, but because the island is long and narrow and resembles a rattler's head at one end. Only three fam-

Rev. William F. Ferguson. He makes his rounds in Island Airlines' Fords. Also a schoolmaster on Middle Bass Island, he commutes daily to class room. (Photo by the author)

Island youngsters fly in the Fords before they can crawl. On this flight mother and baby are doing fine as friend catches shut-eye despite noise of the "Tin Goose." (Island Airlines Photo)

At North Bass Island, (also Isle of St. George) end of the line, Postmistress Mrs. Dorothy Burris picks up the morning mail. Shanty is North Bass "waiting room." (Photo by the author)

ilies live there the year around. The whole island covers less than 85 acres.

Yet Rattlesnake has its own post office, and thousands of pieces of mail are handled every week! The reason is that there are special Rattlesnake Island stamps, triangular issues in a variety of colors. One has a picture of the Ford Trimotor on it, and collectors from all over seek the postmark cancellation.

Mrs. Charles Busch is the postmistress. She and her husband also operate the Golden Pheasant Inn, the only establishment of any size on the island. This is great pheasant country and the population swells with eager nimrods during the season, when the "Pheasant Run" keeps the trimotors flying extra sections.

The runway at Rattlesnake is less than 1500 feet long, and the Fords are the only planes of their size that could operate here with any degree of safety. The terminal building is the Busch Homestead, a large white frame house with a windsock on one of its gables. When we land, hundreds of pheasants scatter in all directions. On take-off, the plane is less than thirty feet in the air when the rock shoreline ends in a steep drop off. Getting in, and getting out is a

High-flying student. She rides Ford trimotor to school every day from outer islands to Put-In-Bay high school. (Island Airlines Photo)

Matriarch of the fleet, Island Airlines' N7584, is 40 years old this year (1968) the 38th trimotor to be turned out at Ford plant in Dearborn. Here, the famed "Tin Goose," oldest of the flying Fords still in daily operation, heads out over her island domain. (Island Airlines Photo)

Harold Hauck, who has more hours in the "Tin Goose" than any other pilot.
(Photo by the author)

"Barnstormer" Milton ("Red") Hershberger, who started Island Airline operation in 1929.
(Photo courtesy Milton Hershberger)

thrill. The trick is the "Tin Goose's" secret.

North Bass Island, the end of the line, is a five minute hop away. Here, when we land, Mrs. Dorothy Burris is waiting to get the morning mail sacks. She's been doing it for eight years, the official mail carrier. This northernmost island before the lake becomes Canadian waters, is famous for its grape harvests. The airport rests among the arbors.

In all, Island Airlines' route covers about 17 miles one way. Pushing the Ford at top cruising speed of about 85-mph, it takes less than 45 minutes to make the round-trip from Port Clinton. That includes twelve landings and take-offs. The plane stops only at Put-in-Bay on its regular scheduled return trip.

"THE SHORTEST AIRLINE IN THE WORLD," it says on the printed timetables.

There are other proud boasts that Island Airlines can make: (1) It owns the 38th Ford 4-AT ever built, License Number N-7584, which to the best of anyone's knowledge, is the oldest Ford Trimotor still flying. (2) In 1966, Dietrick bought a Ford 5-AT (License Number XA-HIL) which is said to have more flying hours to its credit — 23,000 — than any of the Fords still in existence. (3) One of Island Airlines' pilots, Harold Hauck, has over 11,000 hours flying in Fords, a record of sorts. (4) More important, perhaps, is the fact that Island Airlines is the only airline in the world still flying Fords in daily scheduled operations.

This is Ford Country — as the saying goes. *Ford Trimotor country* to be more specific. One of the old, all-metal planes takes off or lands on the average of every ten minutes, year around.

II

THE history of Island Airlines goes back to 1929 when a barn-storming pilot named Milton Hershberger decided he could make a go of an air freight service to the islands. Hershberger started the operation with two Monocoupes, high-wing monoplanes, and some early Waco biplanes. There was also an old five-place Standard — the workhorse — a biplane with an open cockpit in the front which carried four passengers, two abreast seating, facing each other. The pilot sat in a single-place cockpit in the rear. Later, in 1935, Hershberger got a fleet of five Ford Trimotors, and the line became Island Airways. From then on, the "Tin Goose" became a familiar profile in the skies over the island region.

Then, in September of 1953, Ralph Dietrick, who had been running a small airline from Sandusky, Ohio to Kelly's Island and Canada's Pelee Island, negotiated the purchase of the entire island-hopping venture from Hershberger. Dietrick, a World War II flight instructor and air transport command pilot, changed the name to Island Airlines. For a while, until 1962, home base was at Sandusky. Then, the operation was moved to the Municipal Airport at Port Clinton. Dietrick at the same time sold the Kelly's Island and Pelee Island operations.

Hershberger started island-hopping airline with this fleet of planes. At left is three-place Travelaire. In center is five-place Standard, and at right is three-place straight-wing Waco. The airline started operating Ford trimotors in 1935.   (Photo courtesy Milton Hershberger)

Today Island Airlines owns three Ford trimotors, the "big Ford" a 5-AT in foreground and two 4-AT models shown here parked on the ground at Port Clinton base.   (Photo by the author)

Ralph Dietrick, president of Sky Tours, Inc., at the wheel of N7584. (Photo by the author)

Only four of Island Airlines' pilots are qualified to fly the trimotors. This is Jack Marshall at controls. Note gearshift brake and aisle facing seats. (Photo by the author)

Today Island Airlines, the corporate name is SKY TOURS, INC., operates a flying school, an air-taxi charter service, and the island airline service. The airline owns three Ford trimotors (two 4-AT models with seating arrangements for 15 passengers and one 5-AT model, "the Big Ford," which can accommodate 17 passengers, a Boeing 247, 14-passenger, low-wing monoplane (the last of the 1933 airliners which replaced the Ford trimotors on the major trunklines) plus three Cessna 172's, one 206 Cessna, a Mooney Super 21 and a six-passenger Piper Cherokee. The Cessnas, Boeing and the others also fly the airline route, but the big burden rests on the Ford trimotors. They make the operation unique, because nowhere else in the United States are three of the ancient planes still flying from one base.

Island Airlines' Fords park visitors right at the front door of this modern SKYTEL on Put-In-Bay Island. There is swimming pool and restaurant nearby. (Photo by the author)

Ralph Dietrick, dean of all Ford trimotor pilots with 8,000 hours at the controls of the "Tin Goose" poses with student Hal Beck (in plane) at Port Clinton airport. Dietrick has fleet of smaller planes and runs flight training school as well as operating "Shortest Airline In The World."

At this writing, SKY TOURS, INC. employs twenty persons including pilots, office personnel, mechanics, line crews and restaurant personnel. Dietrick is president-manager and pilot. There are five other pilots — Harold Hauck, Newell Witte, Jack Marshall, Dave St. Clair, and Roger Fair. Mechanics are Rodney Lewis, Ed Zilles, Jim Dickson and Larry Mattox. Everybody, pilots included, helps service the planes and handle the loading and unloading of passengers and freight.

There are plans to expand the operation, especially on Put-in-Bay; build a bigger *Skytel* and a bigger restaurant. Dietrick is already in the real estate business, building for sale and renting, cottages on the islands, where he owns many acres as well as the landing strips.

What makes Island Airlines unusual in another aspect, is the very nature of its environment and, of course, the planes it flies. The small group of islands just offshore in the shallowest and second smallest of our Great Lakes is a strange complex.

About 800 permanent residents live on the Islands, but in the summertime vacationists swell the population tenfold. This whole region is a scenic and historic wonderland, a resort paradise.

Put-in-Bay is the center of activities with many thousands making a pilgrimage to Perry's Monument, the second highest shrine in the U. S., next to the Washington Monument. Hotels, cottages and camp sites are located all along its shoreline, and shallow Lake Erie offers some of the finest beaches in the world with the warmest of Great Lakes' waters to attract swimmers. Fishing and other water sports draw enthusiasts from all over the mid-west and Canada.

This is the spawning ground for the famous Lake Erie perch and pickerel, and pan fish are plentiful. Flotillas of small boats filled with anglers can be seen from the air. And in winter-time, even, the ice is covered with shanty-towns. The area is rated by national sports magazines as the third best fresh-water fishing spot in the United States.

A major event each year is the Inter-Lake Regatta, one of the largest held anywhere. Hundreds of sailboats enter the racing competition. The sight of the boats, with their many colored sails, as seen from the flying Fords, is one to behold!

The outer islands offer less in the way of resort attractions, but for campers who want to "rough it," this is the place to go. On Middle Bass, big wineries offer the visitor a chance to see champagne made. Some of the finest domestic spirits come from their great casks.

"The Lake That Flows Red," Erie is

Some say the "Tin Goose" runs on wine, and it is true to a degree. The Lake Erie islands provide some of the finest vineyards anywhere and the wineries are big customers of the airline. Here a group of tourists visit the famous George Lonz winery on Middle Bass Island.   (Port Clinton Chamber of Commerce photo)

At Port Clinton Airport Dietrick runs small restaurant and bar (beer only). Naturally the name of the restaurant could only be as shown here. (Photo by the author)

Only "Tin Goose" flying club in the world is located at Port Clinton base of Island Airlines. This is insignia. Club is social organization. (Island Airlines Photo)

sometimes called, because of its wines and sparkling burgundy. Wine-making is the only industry of the islands, the main reason most permanent residents live there. The wineries offer employment to most of the island populace.

It is probably true, that because of the wineries, the fabulous flying Fords are kept busy the year around. There would likely be little business in the winter time on the outer island route were it not for the villagers.

On the mainland, too, there are major attractions. Near Sandusky is Cedar Point, a recreation pier and boardwalk that is the mid-west's Atlantic City. There is also the famous Blue Hole and its crystal caves at nearby Castalia, Ohio.

And one must not forget the "Tin Goose" as one of the attractions. The antique Fords draw big crowds to the Port Clinton airport.

Their exploits, summer and winter, are legend.

III

THE Ford trimotors that Island Airlines flies are standard models. But seating arrangements are a far cry from the interiors in the first Fords of 40 years ago that went into airline operation. Seats are small, straight-backed, leather-cushioned, bolted down chairs. There is no sound-proofing, just bare metal inside the cabin. Engines, through the years, have improved so much that the planes are quieter today than they were originally. But it's still noisy inside. Open cockpit windows provide ventilation. There is no radio communication, and a minimum of instruments are in the cockpit.

Outwardly, the planes have a distinctive look; Island's paint job is white with red and blue trimmings. The "Big Ford" (the 5-AT) is silver with red and blue markings.

There is still a lot of "barnstorming" that goes on, but for the most part the planes are too busy flying the line. Published timetables show an average of five scheduled flights a day, six days a week, with nine flights on Saturdays. When the traffic gets too heavy, as it does at peak vacation times and during ice fishing and hunting seasons, extra sections are added.

Someone has pointed out, it may well be that Island Airlines originated the idea of the "shuttle plane service" which some of the major carriers now use on routes such as between Washington-New York, San Diego-Los Angeles-San Francisco.

Certainly Island's boarding technique is similar to the shuttle operations. There is no reservations system. Passengers just show up, ready to board about ten minutes before flight time. There is a full-time ticket office at Port Clinton and South Bass, but on the other islands you get your ticket from the pilot. A round-trip to South Bass

Nothing fancy, just raw airplane, but passengers love to ride in the "Tin Goose." Airline runs many special sightseeing trips during peak season in summer months. This planeload is occupied with scenery.
(Photo by the author)

Harriet Martin, Island Airlines' "Girl Friday," veteran of 13 years with Sky Tours, Inc.
(Photo by the author)

costs $4.00 which compares with $2.50 by ferryboat. The plane takes about five minutes, the boat about an hour. The airline offers a special rate during August on Mondays when traffic is light — $2.50 round-trip to South Bass. Mostly, the cut-rate is to stimulate sight-seeing trips.

Passengers who board the Fords can carry on just about anything of reasonable size and weight without charge. There is one commuter, weight about 300 pounds, (he takes up two spaces on the side-long bench seats up front) who once a week visits the mainland and takes back with him several suitcases of whiskey. Total weight — about 500 pounds for a $3.50 ticket. Nobody complains.

"He's one of our regulars," Ralph laughs it off.

Freight rates are unbelievingly low, almost ridiculous. For non-perishable goods it's one cent a pound; a cent-and-a-quarter

Island Airlines "big Ford" at right is capable of carrying 17-passengers. Behind the trimotor is Boeing 247-D, the type which first replaced the Fords on the airlines in the '30s. Until 1968 Island Airlines owned this Boeing, one of the last known to be in existence.
(Photo by the author)

a pound for perishables. On large shipments, like a refrigerator or a TV console, which involve special handling in loading, there is a flat additional charge of one dollar.

Weight and balance is a problem with the Fords which can carry a maximum of about 4,000 pounds payload. Island Airlines has its own, rather unusual, weight control and passenger priority system. When you buy a ticket you get a small metal tag (about theater ticket size) which identifies your flight by color — red, blue, yellow. The first plane out, for instance, is *blue flight*. There are only 15 seats, so they pass out only 15 blue tags. That way, the flight is never oversold. At the same time, blue tag holders get to board first, then reds, and yellows, a kind of check-and-balance on a first-come, first-served basis. Pilots collect the metal tag at the door of the plane.

Passengers also get a small yellow ticket with a picture of the Ford Trimotor on it. On the ticket it says — "Souvenir of your flight on THE SHORTEST AIRLINE IN THE WORLD aboard a Ford Trimotor".

Business is booming. In 1967, the airline carried a record number of more than 65,000 passengers. Freight averages about 300,000 pounds a year, plus 150,000 pounds of mail.

Conversely, operational costs are also skyrocketing. It costs about $40.00 an hour to fly, maintain, and cover insurance on the Fords. That's pretty reasonable considering on peak Sundays, with the three trimotors and the Boeing shuttling back and forth to South Bass, alone, they have carried up to 250 passengers an hour. But Harriet Martin, Sky Tours' secretary for 13 years, will tell you that upkeep of the runways, hangars, shops and other facilities on the ground, eats into the profits faster than the Fords burn up their 80-octane gasoline. There's more to it than profit or loss.

"It's a good feeling," Ralph declares,

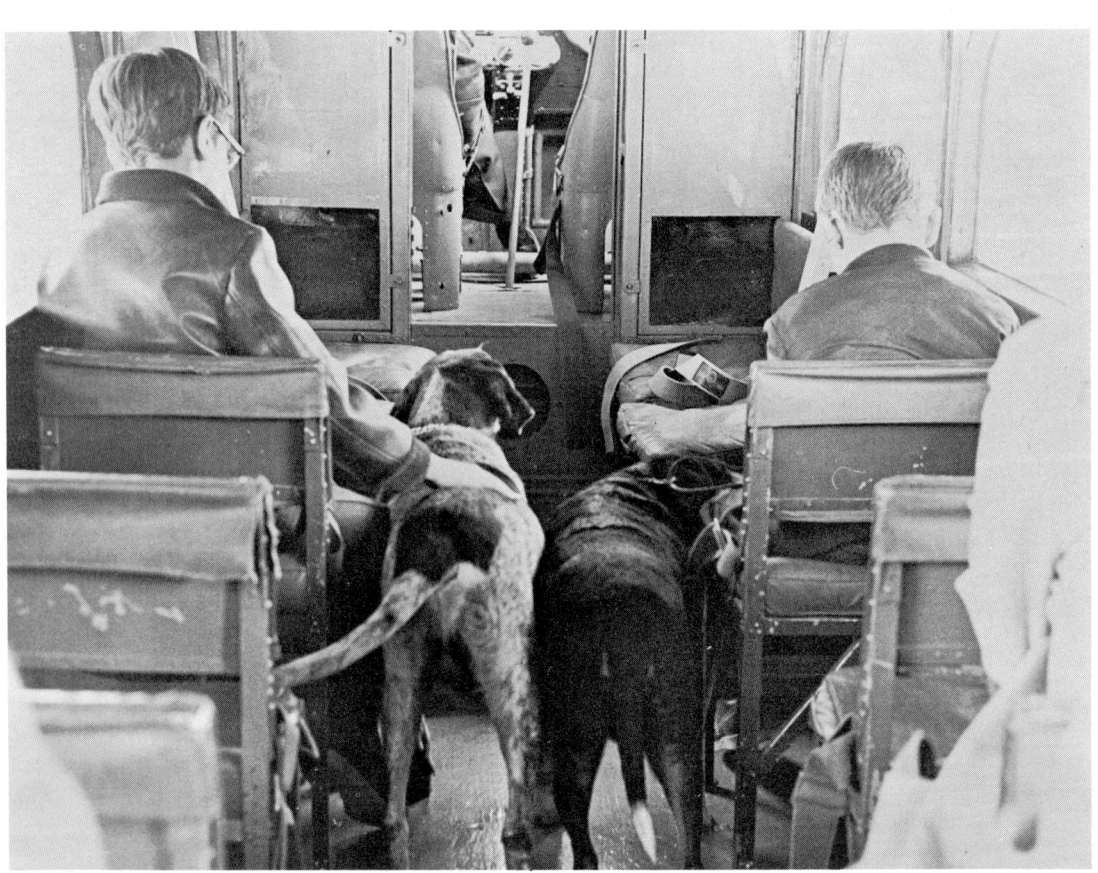

Pets are frequent "commuters". Note type seats which permit carrying 13 passengers in 4-AT models, twelve in main cabin, and one up front in co-pilot's seat. (Island Airlines Photo)

Erie Islands offer some of the best pheasant hunting anywhere. This group on special charter trip to Pelee Island, a Canadian possession, has just passed customs inspection. The bird "kill" speaks for itself. Island Airlines at one time had regular service to Kellys Island and to Pelee, now discontinued.
(Photo by Harley W. Hoffman)

"to know that the airline is providing a vital service to the people of the islands. Without it a lot of things wouldn't be the way they are."

The truth is, if it weren't for Island Airlines a lot of people wouldn't have jobs, so it helps the economy. Likewise, it would affect the resort business. Revenues derived from fishermen and hunters would decrease. The kids couldn't get to school in the winter time. Dr. Heinz Boker, M.D. couldn't make his weekly visits to the islands from the mainland. A lot of people would be robbed of vacation pleasures.

Mrs. Irene Lent, who operates a vacation resort and Inn at Put-in-Bay, sums it up in this fashion: "If we run out of ice cubes, as it sometimes happens, we just call up Ralph or Harriet or somebody. They crank up a plane and fly the ice over in a matter of minutes. Folks in our neck-of-the woods wouldn't know what to do if the Fords stopped flying."

Island housewives are also grateful for a special "super market service" that Island Airlines provides.

Here's the way it works: When Mom, who lives on Middle Bass, for instance, wants the week's groceries, she picks up the phone and calls the airline at Port Clinton, and reads off her shopping list. A shuttle bus goes to the market and fills the order which goes out on the next trip. There is a 25 cent delivery charge. Likewise, on the early morning flight pilots often pick up the grocery lists at the island stops. On return trips, throughout the day, the flyboys play grocery boys.

Somebody once quipped about Island's operation — "Long on service, short on routes."

In addition to foodstuffs, the Fords haul just about anything and everything. Pets, feed, reels of barbed wire, machinery, medicines, fresh-caught fish are other items. Stories, some of them almost unbelievable, abound about the variety of cargoes.

During one winter, for instance, ice coated the power cables to one of the islands. An emergency generator had to be used to supply electricity until the cable

Fords provide unique "Flying Funeral" Service.   *(Truck-Tractor Equipment Co. Photo)*

was repaired. To feed the generator, the Fords hauled 4,000 gallons of fuel oil in fifty-gallon drums.

Another time, a fireplug in Put-in-Bay broke. A new one, weighing 500 pounds was flown in, and that part of the village was without fire protection for only a matter of hours.

When a boatyard on Middle Bass needed a king-size piece of timber which was twenty feet long, Ralph figured out a way to deliver it, even though at first, it wouldn't fit into the Ford's cabin. They stuck one end in the cockpit, and let the other end stick out from the open door in the rear.

"She flew perfectly," Ralph reported.

There is also a "flying funeral service."

When there is a death on the islands, the Fords haul the deceased and the entire funeral party to mainland cemeteries. One funeral required five trips to accommodate the whole party.

A favorite story pilots like to tell is about the man, who refused to fly because there was a casket and tombstone on board. "I won't ride with anything like that," the passenger declared. "It's a bad omen." To oblige, they rolled out another Ford and flew him, alone, to Middle Bass.

There was another time, the airline would have been better off if it had refused to fly one shipment. They got a call from one of the wineries that a big shipment was coming by motor freight to the home base at Port Clinton. Important! Rush! When the shipment arrived, it was so bulky that it filled up the entire airplane. They had to shuttle back and forth half a day to complete delivery. The airline really lost money that day. The shipment didn't weigh much. It consisted of huge cardboard cartons of corks for champagne and wine bottles. Total weight — less than 500 pounds. Total revenue — less than $5.00.

That's the way it is, day in and day out, around Island Airlines where the "Tin

On Middle Bass Island Fords operate from grass field, no paved runway. Here a group of passengers transfers from one plane to another, permitting North Bass passengers to continue on to end of line, while other Ford returns to mainland to pick up more waiting passengers for Put-in-Bay. Dispatcher at Port Clinton shuffles plans around to cut costs and run more efficient schedules. (Island Airlines Photo)

Goose" still flies in all kinds of weather.

For the amount of flying it does, its up-and-down landings and take-offs, the line has a remarkable safety record. There has never been a fatality in all the years of operation.

Once, an engine tore loose and dropped off, but the plane turned around and landed safely. Another time, one of the planes landed on the ice to pick up some stranded fishermen. The ice broke and the plane sank, but it, too, was recovered and flew again.

Much of the safety record is attributed to the fact that the Fords are rugged and tough and built for the workhorse duty. Another factor is that Island Airlines' Ford pilots altogether have over 25,000 hours of flying the trimotors, proof of their proficiency. They know their machines, inside and out. And they love to fly, especially the Fords. They treat the trimotors much like an antique car buff coddles his 40-year old Cadillac, Model-T or Overland. Mechanics feel the same way; the Fords are pampered, polished and petted.

IV

THIS unusual airline, like any other scheduled passenger carrier must operate under strict safety rules and regulations. But Island Airlines, because of the nature of its route structure and the planes it flies, has special regulatory consideration. It is permitted to fly with one mile visibility and 500-foot ceiling which, admittedly, with faster and larger planes would be cutting things a little close. But the fact is, the Fords seldom climb above 500 feet. The island landing fields are so close together, the plane is barely airborne when it is making ready for its landing. With their big wing for support, they could glide to safety. Fog is the big "grounder," but the stuff usually comes and goes in a hurry, so there aren't many long delays.

"We have an unfailing yardstick for the weather," Ralph explains. "When we can

Wine-maker, George Lonz checks manifest with Newell Witte, veteran Ford pilot. The cargo speaks for itself. (Island Airlines Photo)

75

Island Airlines is year-around operation, but in winter months schedules are cut to about three round-trips a day. Here N7584 takes off from snow covered field at Put-in-Bay. Planes probably make more take-offs and landings than any other airline operation. (Island Airlines Photo)

see the top of Perry's monument, that's ceiling enough. We can go."

In the last ten years, he points out with pride, there have been only ten days when schedules had to be cancelled because of bad weather.

The Fords never fly at night, unless it is an emergency.

The secret, according to Dietrick, is that the Fords are made to order for this particular operation. "They are just what we need," Ralph declares. "They seem to relish on the wear and tear, and they require little maintenance. Controls or cables are all outside and easy to inspect. It's the same way with the engines, and the metal surfaces are tough as a tin roof. I've never heard of one being overloaded; they can lift anything that will fit inside. Speed is something they don't have, and we don't need. Nobody yet, as far as we know, has ever worn one out."

Newell Witte, who has been flying the Fords for years and at one time managed the airline for Dietrick at Port Clinton when the operation was based in Sandusky, puts it another way. "The only trouble is this thing gets a little monotonous," he says. "It's like driving a bus."

Glancing back at a cabin filled with strange cargo, he adds with a big grin — "Maybe, I should say, driving a truck."

Mechanics feel about the same way regarding their charges. Veteran crew chief, Rodney Lewis says, "We run this thing like a garage. Every night the planes get a thorough inspection, and if anything needs fixin' we do it right here in our own shops. The toughest job is getting the fish smell out of the cabin."

The Fords get pampered. When slightest thing goes wrong, into the shops they go, even if it means getting a skin-grafting job.
(Photo by the author)

Machine shop at Port Clinton hangar. (Photo by the author)

Chief Mechanic Rodney Lewis checks "Tin Goose" powerplant. (Photo by the author)

Engine maintenance is almost too simple. At the end of World War II, Island Airlines bought more than a hundred surplus engines. They are stored in the hangar at Put-in-Bay. When something serious develops, mechanics simply yank out the engine, and put in a new one. A giant pile of burned out engines in another hangar at Port Clinton has thousands of useable spare parts to take care of minor engine repairs.

Nor is there any shortage of airframe parts. In the beginning when Island got its first Fords, Hershberger with farsightedness bought up a reserve supply of ailerons, rudders, fins and corrugated skin — a priceless cache today in the rafters and corners of the hangars, wherever storage space is available.

"We've got enough engines and spare airframe parts to go on for another fifteen years or longer, "Ralph confides. "The old 'Tin Goose' has a lot of life ahead of her yet."

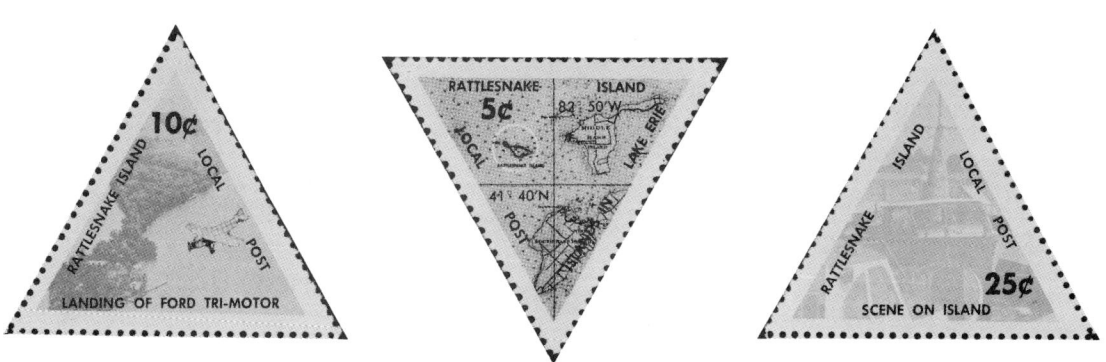

In the middle of the Jet Age, there are still twelve of the famous Ford trimotors listed by the Federal Aviation Agency as being in flyable condition. Three of them are owned by Island Airlines at Port Clinton, Ohio. Shown here, two of the smaller 4-AT's make a fly-over in salute to their big sister, the 5-AT on the ground. The plane in back of Big Ford is a Boeing 247-D, the type that replaced the Fords on the airlines in the 1930s.

(Photo by the Author)

CHAPTER FIVE

The Second Time Around

ONE day back in 1964 Gaylord Moxon, who runs Moxon Electronics Corporation of Santa Monica, California and his pretty, brunette wife, Grace, were flying in their private plane over the rolling terrain of Idaho. Suddenly, below, they spotted a dilapidated "Tin Goose' parked in a field. Moxon, who also runs Mox-Air, which collects and refurbishes vintage aircraft of famous breeds like the Lockheed *Vega*, Fairchild "71," Ryan B-1, Curtiss Robin, Standard biplane and others, when he saw the old Ford, immediately landed in the cow pasture airport to take a closer look.

The plane was for real, all right, and flyable, but it wasn't any ravishing beauty in its then state of condition. Stripped down inside with big tanks in its cabin and tubes sticking out, here and there, with a few birds nest thrown in, she was being used as a crop sprayer. Its owner, Eugene Frank, was a little reluctant, but "Mox" talked him into selling the prized possession. Today it is one of the dozen or so Ford trimotors known to be in existence and still flying, a model 5-AT-B that was built in March, 1929.

"The best information we can get on its history," Moxon relates, "is that it was originally sold to Transcontinental Air Transport and was used in the 1929 air-rail service experiment, the first coast-to-coast all-passenger operation. When TWA (successor to TAT) phased out its trimotor operations, the plane, License Number N-9651, was sold to the Radio Corporation of America and was all plushed-up as an executive aircraft.

"Next we find N-9651 in Klondike skies flying with Alaskan Airlines. It was there that Eugene Frank spotted it and when he bought it, the plane made an historic journey. Frank trucked the plane down the Alcan Highway to Caldwell, Idaho where he put it to work as a crop duster and sometimes as a barnstormer.

"We bought it from Gene, who confessed it had really been just sitting in the field for quite sometime."

When Moxon brought the ship to the big Mox-Air hangar at Clover Field, Santa Monica, his mechanics turned the rugged, old "Tin Goose" into a peacock. The cabin interior was restored with wood paneling just like the original "airliner" of the thirties, same seats, same cockpit, same instruments, rebuilt engines, but everything possible from original parts. To give N-9651 her "new look", more than 6000 man hours were required. But she is once more a proud queen of the skies.

The plane is bright and shining in its all-metal dress with blue trimmings. It is used strictly for exhibition purposes and barnstorming, carrying passengers for sightseeing flights. Capable of carrying 15 passengers in the leather-upholstered, metallic chairs of 1929 vintage or exact replicas, N-9651 does well at $6.00 a head for adults, $3.00 for children on short flights over the city. Passengers get a souvenir ticket with a picture of the plane on it and the words — *"I Flew In The Original Ford Tri-Motor N-9651."*

The name of the plane, incidentally, is "Graceful". And that's the way she flies!

"We don't have any trouble getting passengers," Moxon says. "The 'Tin Goose' seems to have a magnetism that attracts crowds."

As late as September 18, 1967 on the occasion of the 40th anniversary of the Port of Oakland, the plane was flown from Oak-

Low and slow, but it's a thrill to fly in the 40-year-old trimotor, and Moxon's N9651 is one of the most beautiful of the remaining flyable Fords. Plane is named "Graceful" after Grace Moxon, who was with her husband when they spotted the ancient Ford in Idaho cow pasture.   (Photo courtesy Mox-Air, Inc.)

land International Airport on sight-seeing trips. But even on the ground, she was the center of attraction. Amid static displays of space vehicles, helicopters, jet airliners, military fighters and bombers, the ancient Ford trimotor drew large crowds.

"She is a living legend," Moxon says, "Perhaps, that is the reason for all the attention."

There are other Fords still flying besides this one and the three owned by Island Airlines. One is owned by Harrah's Automobile Collection (HAC) of Reno, Nevada.

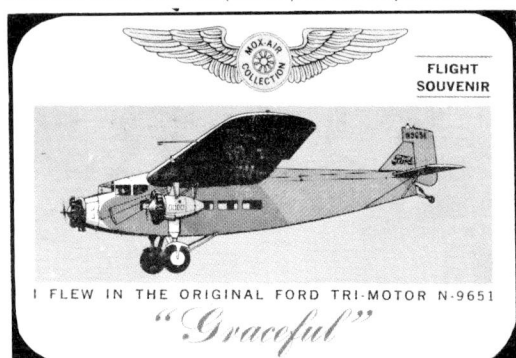

*Moxon's Ford takes up hundreds of aviation buffs who want to ride in the trimotor. This is souvenir ticket each passenger receives.
(Photo Courtesy Mox-Air, Inc.)*

The HAC "Tin Goose" is a 5-AT model, the eighth of the big Fords to come off the line at the Stout factory in Dearborn. First flown December 1, 1928, it was delivered to NAT in 1929 with the registration NC9645, and later that year to TAT where it was in service until 1931. It flew for TWA and then Grand Canyon Airlines until 1937, when it disappeared for a time, appearing in 1942 in Nicaragua. The wandering plane then went to Mexico where it had several owners and a new Mexican registration XB-NET, issued in 1950 as the plane was not used commercially. In February 1951 XB-NET was completely overhauled by Torres Landa in the Servicios Aeronauticos de Mexico S.A. shops, and in late 1951 it was flown again after major repairs. It was at this time that the trimotor received a new sheet dural skin, replacing the original corrugated type, making it the only "smooth-skinned" Ford trimotor in existence.

HAC bought the plane several years ago and flew it from Boise, Idaho to its new home among other proud vintage vehicles at Reno, Nevada. It is currently under restoration and soon will take its rightful place in the skies.

Unique on this Ford trimotor is the smooth skin, a present-day sheet dural, replacing the original corrugated covering which was synonymous with all other Fords. It was applied after a major overhaul in Mexico in 1951. (Photo courtesy Harrah's Automobile Collection, Reno, Nevada)

One of the Johnson Flying Service Fords working with the U.S. Forestry Service, drops "smoke jumpers" into fire area, part of fire retardation and soil conservation program. Smoke jumpers helped fight big Sun Dance fire of 1967, one of the worst conflagrations to hit northwest region.
(Photo Courtesy Johnson Flying Service/Missoulian Sentinel)

The Johnson Flying Service of Missoula, Montana still owns and operates two of the Ford trimotors. Here, Bob Johnson, president, is shown with one of the Fords which is used primarily in forest spraying and fire-spotting operations. Johnson is standing in 1923 Ford Model-T run about.
(Photo courtesy Johnson Flying Service)

The Johnson Flying Service of Missoula, Montana owns two more of the flyable trimotors which are used almost exclusively, working with the U.S. Forestry Service in fire retardation and soil conservation programs. In the fall of 1967, when one of the worst timber fires in history hit the Sun Dance Forest region of Idaho, they were first on the scene parachuting in men and equipment to help fight the inferno.

"Each of the Fords can carry eight smoke jumpers and their gear," Johnson's chief pilot, Jack Hughes explained. "They also are used for timber spraying and aerial grass-seeding, their stripped-down interiors fitted with ingenuous tanks, bins and blowers."

Says Robert R. Johnson, owner of the Missoula operation: "For this kind of flying there never was, and probably never will be a better aircraft ever built."

Meanwhile, Ford Trimotor, Inc. of Ottawa, Kansas, in 1967, was reported to be operating one of the venerable old workhorses used for crop dusting and exhibition flying at county fairs and air shows. There are said to be others still flying in Mexico and South America. It is possible there are more scattered in remote areas of the globe that are unreported.

"From time to time one is advertised for sale in the classified columns of the aviation magazines," says Island Airlines' Ralph Dietrick. "They vanish, and then, suddenly, reappear again, a habit the 'Tin

Johnson Flying Service Ford showing special chemical spray device beneath wing used in soil conservation activity.
(Photo Courtesy Johnson Flying Service)

Goose' probably picked up from the feathered specie."

The remarkable thing is that the winged thunderbirds Henry Ford built when the Model-T was the only car the Ford Motor Company produced, are still around. The Indestructibles!

II

THE *NOW* GENERATION must also include some of the Ford trimotors several major airlines are still flying although not in scheduled operations. It is, in a way, a strange paradox. Remember, in the early

Another of remaining Ford Trimotors is owned by Ford Trimotor, Inc. of Ottawa, Kansas. Plane is a 4-AT model used for barnstorming. Here it is shown about to become airborne. *(Ed Wojtas Photo)*

Commemorating the 20th anniversary of the first TAT coast-to-coast, all-passenger service in 1929, TWA leased old N7584 from Island Airlines (then, Island Air Service) and flew it over original route. Plane is shown here on ramp at Port Clinton, Ohio prior to delivery to TWA pilots.   (Island Airlines Photo)

thirties, it was the airlines that "took" to the all-metal Fords, and made them the sky queens of the commercial airways. It was also the airlines in later years, that gave the planes a second lease on life, when they recaptured those early days of air travel in a series of commemorative anniversary flights. In each production, elaborately staged, the "Tin Goose" was the star performer.

Trans World Airlines started the trend in 1949 celebrating the 20th anniversary of its first transcontinental air service. TWA leased one of the Fords from Island Airlines (then Island Air Service), painted it with the original markings of TAT (Transcontinental Air Transport) and flew the plane over the route which TAT pioneered 20 years before.

Again in 1963, commemorating the 25th anniversary of the Civil Aeronautics Act, TWA chartered another Ford and flew it coast-to-coast with special press group on

On the 25th anniversary of the Civil Aeronautics Act of 1938, TWA leased another Ford Trimotor and flew it coast-to-coast on special press flight. Plane is shown here shortly after take-off from LA International Airport on start of journey.   (Trans World Airlines Photo)

The "Tin Goose" is always center of attraction wherever it goes. Here's proof — Northwest's 30th Anniversary Ford trimotor parked on ramp along with vintage 1956 four-engined Douglas DC-6, Convair 440 and DC-3s (top left) Note plane has Northwest Airways, Inc. markings of 1926 when NWA started operations Northwest originally purchased Plane N8419 in 1929. (Northwest Orient Airlines Photo)

board. One writer described flight as — "the last gasp of the Tin Goose."

Ironically, the plane N414H is still flying. It is today owned by American Airlines, Inc. and is hangared at Tulsa Oklahoma shops of the airline.

As a result of the favorable press and public acceptance of the TWA 20th anniversary flight, other airlines followed suit with similar flights commemorating the introduction of air service to cities along their routes. The old Fords, some of which had been relegated to a variety of not very glamorous missions, suddenly found themselves proud "Sky Queens" once more in an era of turbo-props and turbo-jet airliners.

Northwest Orient Airlines dusted off one of the old Fords and used it for an anniversary celebration. The plane, NC-8419, a 5-AT which Northwest Airways (a forerunner company) had purchased in 1929 was leased from Johnson Flying Service in 1956 (Johnson then had five Fords in operation) and appeared all plumed-up in Northwest Airways gleaming white with original distinctive markings. She was destined to make history of a sort.

On October 9, 1956 a crowd gathered at Idlewild Airport, Long Island (now Kennedy International) and there were appropriate ceremonies explaining this was the 30th anniversary of NWA. Appropriately, veteran Northwest pilots, Captain L. S. "Deke" DeLong and Captain Joe Kimm both of whom had flown Ford Trimotors in the early thirties for the airline, took their positions in the cockpit of NC-8419 for the start of a long journey, city-hopping across the U.S.

"The purpose of this flight," said the master of ceremonies, "is to illustrate the tremendous advances of commercial aviation since the airline was founded in October of 1926 . . .

"The Ford trimotor has been selected because it was this type of airplane that proved commercial air carrier operations over the Rocky Mountains were safe. A flight of a Ford trimotor from the Twin

Ford trimotor N9683 played unusual role in reincarnation of the "Tin Goose" which emerged as "Bushmaster 2000." Hayden sold plane to American Airlines and this is the way it looked after complete refurbishing job in airline's Tulsa, Oklahoma shops. Note original American Airways markings, insignia for predecessor company of today's vast American Airlines' system. In 1930s American Airways owned this same plane, flew it coast-to-coast. (American Airlines Photo)

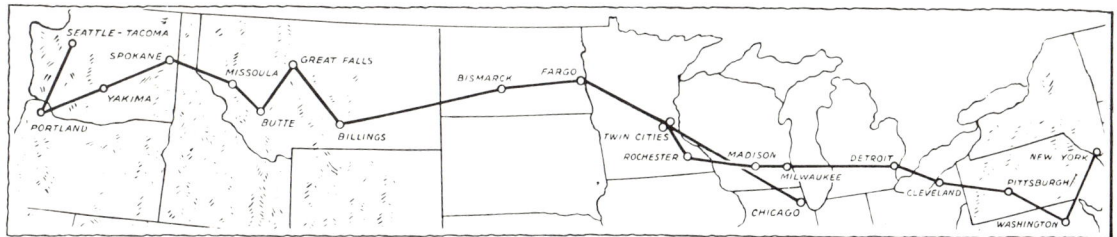
Route of Northwest 30th Anniversary Ford trimotor across U.S.

Cities (Minneapolis-St. Paul, Minnesota, home base for Northwest) to Seattle in 1933 helped win for the airline the northern transcontinental route."

With that, the Ford took off for Washington, D. C. first stop on its cross-country venture. Thence, for the next nine days, it made stops at Pittsburgh, Cleveland, Detroit, Milwaukee, Chicago, Madison, Rochester, Minn., Minneapolis-St. Paul, Fargo, Bismarck, Billings, Great Falls, Butte, Missoula, Spokane, Yakima and Portland — all terminal points on Northwest's system.

High tribute to the airplane was paid at Seattle-Tacoma Airport when a throng of spectators turned out in a driving rain to welcome the "Tin Goose".

The plane went back to work with Johnson Flying Service, with its wire-spoke wheels and other original features.

Seven years later, in 1962, American Airlines also got into the act of putting the spotlight on the Fords, when they bought 5-AT-39 (N9683) which they had originally operated three decades before.

According to American Airlines, this Ford was built in April, 1929 and first sold to Southwest Air Fast Express (SAFE) of Tulsa, Oklahoma. Eighteen months later it was bought by SAFE of Delaware and the next year, in May of 1931 was sold to Colonial Air Transport, Inc. of Newark, New Jersey. The old American Airways, predecessor of American Airlines bought it in 1933, and the newly organized American Airlines became the owner in February of 1935. It was used on one of American's first transcontinental operations.

In 1936, when American Airlines began operation of the DC-2's and DC-3's the plane was sold to the Aviation Manufacturing Corporation of Chicago. AMCO sold it to Transportes Aeros Centro Americanos, Lt. (TACA) for Central America operations.

For seven years it flew TACA's rough and rugged routes and was then transferred to operations in Nicaragua. In 1946, it was sold to an individual Miguel A. Zuniga of Mexico City, who sold it almost immediately to Carlos Devalos, and for seven years operated it as an airliner in South America.

It was heard from again in 1953 operated by Robert W. Waltermire of Choteau, Montana under a new registration N-1124N, as a crop duster for Northwest Agricultural Aviation. Four years later it was back in Mexico again, flying for a mine operation. When it was advertised for sale in late 1957 Henry Messer of Houston, Texas bought it and once more the faithful old workhorse had an American registration.

Before the end of 1957 it was sold to Hayden Aircraft Corporation of Bellflower, California. There, the plane was given its original registration number N-9683. It was sold to American Airlines in 1962 and ear-marked for posterity.

American Airlines took delivery of the plane at Los Angeles International Airport on September 7, 1962. An American Airlines press release described the occasion: "The tarnished Ford trimotor landed and taxied slowly past the new, ultra-modern satellite buildings and continued on to our maintenance facility. Doubtless, many of the people waiting to board sleek jetliners were bewildered at the sight of this vintage aircraft. None could have guessed that it would very likely fly again."

Those who guessed it wouldn't, were dead wrong. American flew the plane to its Tulsa, Oklahoma over-haul shops. There, it was completely refurbished and emerged an exact replica in minute detail of the original American Airline's Ford Trimotor of the early thirties. It became, and still is at this writing, one of the most beautiful of the few remaining flying Fords.

Early model Ford Trimotors brought unusual profile and fuselage configuration to aircraft design. Noticeable features were the barn-door-like rudder, sharp-pointed tail surfaces, oval-shaped door, thick wing, control cables and "horn" located on outside of fuselage. Skin covering was entirely of corrugated metal.
(Island Airlines Photo)

Millions of people across the U. S. have seen it flying and had opportunity to inspect it on the ground at air shows and other gatherings. Thousands also have been taken for courtesy rides.

"Put one of our Ford trimotors alongside one of our trimotor Astrojets," explained an American Airlines' public relations man, "and the 'Goose' will draw the crowds everytime. It's a great promotional gimmick!"

On a sponsored "barnstorming" tour American flew the plane 1200 hours and more than 130,000 miles. And she will probably keep on flying until the National Air Museum, part of the great Smithsonian Institution in Washington, D.C. is completed where she will have a place of honor along with other such greats as Lindbergh's "Spirit of St. Louis," the first Wright Aeroplane and many others.

So pleased was American Airlines with the public acceptance of its N-9683 that the airline purchased another Ford Trimotor in 1965, dressed it up in 1930 markings and

"Bushmaster 2000," Jet Age version of the Ford Trimotor shows close resemblance to original profile. Note change in tail surfaces, additional dorsal fin and different door shape. Plane also has smooth skin around nose, and all control cables are inside fuselage.
(Photo by Henry Artof)

One of early model Ford trimotors, vintage 1930. Plane was fitted with Pratt & Whitney "Wasp" engines developing about 900 total horsepower. Note ring cowlings on outboard engines were standard equipment for most airliner versions of the 5-AT models. (Trans World Airlines Photo)

The "Bushmaster 2000" an experimental modern day version of the "Tin Goose" is shown here in similar view (with above photo) showing how things have changed. "Bushmaster" has three-bladed full-feathering propellers, full cowlings on all three engines developing over 1200 horsepower. (Photo by Henry Artof)

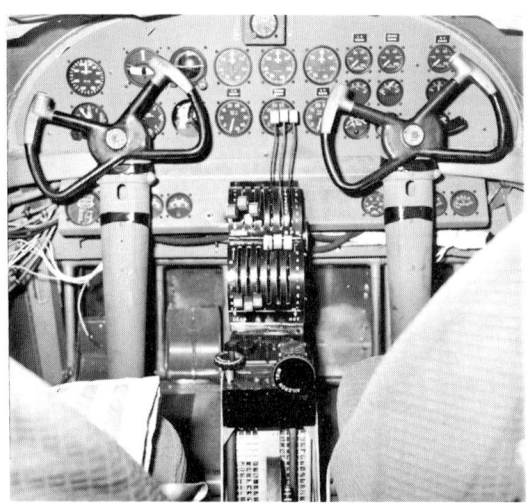

Cockpit instrument panel and controls in "Bushmaster 2000" are far cry from original "Tin Goose" cockpit. Yoke-type control column and throttles are vintage 1968. Plane is equipped with latest radio, engine, fuel, flight and navigational instruments.
(Photo by Henry Artof)

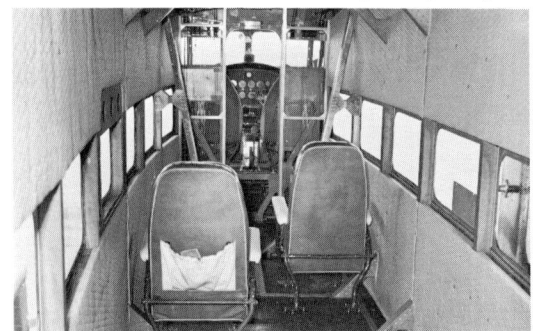

Interior view of "Bushmaster 2000." This is experimental version but in one configuration ship can carry 26 skytroopers. Plane is soundproofed. *(Photo by Henry Artof)*

Laurent "Frenchy" Savard, who probably did more to complete "Bushmaster 2000" experiment model, examines the revolving tail-wheel which is big improvement over original tail skid on first Ford trimotors.
(Photo by Henry Artof)

put it on exhibition at the World's Fair. It now reposes in the hangar at Tulsa awaiting any assignment, probably in reserve to do some more "barnstorming" when N9683 retires to her museum spot.

But let's go back for a minute in time to the role that N9683 played during her brief period at Hayden Aircraft in California.

In the mid-fifties, a small group of individuals, who worked in California's vast aircraft manufacturing complex, got together and formed the Hayden Aircraft Corporation, Robert E. Hayden, President. Many people were surprised when Hayden revealed that William B. Stout, still active in aviation, although aging in years, would be director of engineering for the new corporation.

A few days later, Stout startled everybody by announcing that they were going to start producing the Ford trimotors again. The "Tin Goose" was being resurrected.

Because of his previous connection with The Ford Motor Company, Stout was able to obtain many of the original drawings from which the first 5-AT Ford trimotor was produced. With these, and the help of the younger aeronautical engineers at Hayden, he started re-designing the basic 5-AT, taking advantage of Jet Age "know-how" and technology. The "new" Ford was to be known as THE STOUT BUSHMASTER.

III

THE prototype of the aircraft was to have been completed in 1957, and much of the engineering was, in fact, finished right on schedule. But the project suffered many setbacks. Bill Stout died suddenly in 1956, and everything was up in the air. Hayden Aircraft faded out of the picture.

There were those still interested, however, and they decided to revive the plan to build the modern version of the "Tin Goose." Laurent Eugene "Frenchy" Savard, an old Ford pilot and an original Hayden stockholder was one of those determined to keep the project alive. Another was Ralph Williams, president of Aircraft Hydro-forming Corporation of Gardena, California engaged in manufacturing many parts for the big jumbo jets. Savard and Williams had worked together in the past at the Douglas Aircraft Company in Long

Special feature of "New" Ford is this extra large door to accommodate loading of heavy equipment and good egress for paratroopers.
(Photo by Henry Artof)

One noticeable difference in external configuration between "Tin Goose" and the new "Bushmaster 2000" is the change in empennage. Original Ford barn-door like rudder is gone and more dorsal fin has been added.
(Photo by Henry Artof)

Beach, and they picked up the project where Stout left off, determined to give the "Tin Goose" a kind of re-incarnation.

It was in 1957-58, Savard recalls, that N-9683 came into the picture. "After Stout died," Savard says, "we ran into all kinds of troubles because many of the drawings for specific parts were missing. Try as we might we couldn't locate them, anywhere. So, as an alternative, we decided to buy one of the old Fords, study the parts we needed, and make our own drawings from the original . . .

"It wasn't easy to find one of the old birds for sale. But we finally located N-9683 in Mexico. When we first took a look at it, the plane was sitting on cement blocks, and a Mexican family of five was living in it. But the thing was all intact, wings and engines and everything in its original state.

"The next thing we heard was that the plane had been purchased by somebody in Houston and it was for sale again. That's when we bought it and we went down to Mexico, made it flyable, and flew it back to Long Beach Airport.

"There we virtually took it apart piece by piece and put it back together again. In the process, we got all the detailed information we needed to complete our drawings for the proposed STOUT BUSHMASTER.

"After that we kept the plane for a while and did some barnstorming with it. Then, we sold it to American Airlines."

Meanwhile, for the next three or four years, Savard, Williams and others, squeezing their work effort on THE BUSHMASTER in between a thousand other projects, long hours of overtime and nightwork, finally finished the preliminary engineering phase for the new Ford.

At the same time, in the shops at Aircraft Hydro-Forming, Inc. parts began to take shape. "We bootlegged time, labor and machines," is the way Savard put it. "At one time we had three Navajo Indians working on the project."

"There were a lot of skeptics," says Ralph Williams. "But we were determined to get this thing on the road and make good our claims that the basic Ford design still had a role in this new air age. Our belief was and is, that it can do some jobs better than any other aircraft . . ."

"We got it on the road, all right," reminiscences "Frenchy" Savard. "One day in early 1966 at 3:00 A. M. we trucked the completed fuselage and inboard wing panels down the freeway to the airport at Long Beach. The wings and engines followed, and we did the final assembly work in a big hangar at Aero Center there."

When THE BUSHMASTER 2000 (they changed the name) was finally completed and rolled out onto the ramp, she was a sight to behold. In profile, there was no question she was a Ford Trimotor. But a closer look showed many changes and improvements.

Noticeable was a different rudder shape, more fin and a slightly changed profile. There was still the thick, high-lift airfoil, but the plan form of the wing was changed with a new aileron and tip configuration. But the wing had about the same dimen-

There were skeptics who said the "Bushmaster 2000" would never fly. But here she is at Long Beach Airport, warming up for initial test flight. At right, the "Bushmaster 2000" proudly wings her way above the complex freeway system near Long Beach. In spring of 1968 plane had more than 70 hours in the air.
(Photos by Henry Artof)

sions. The fuselage was higher and wider with a king-size door. Engines were new Pratt & Whitney 450-hp (R-985's) almost double the original power and they were housed in more streamlined nacelles. Inside, she was changed, too, with a much roomier cabin, a modern cockpit with yoke-type controls and new instrument panel with the latest flight and navigational instruments. All control cables were inside the fuselage, unlike on the original Fords.

This was the BUSHMASTER 2000, the plane the skeptics said would never be built. But there she was.

There was only one question now — *would she fly?*

One day in August, 1966, they got the answer. With "Frenchy" Savard, Bob Lanley, president of Catalina Channel Airlines, and famed test pilot Bill Bridgeman aboard, the BUSHMASTER 2000 took off from Long Beach airport and flew to Chino Airport about 50 miles to the north.

"We were very pleased with the initial test," says Bill Bridgeman.

The FAA pronounced the plane airworthy and safe and gave it an experimental ticket to fly back to Long Beach.

There, more work was done on the plane for the next 15 months, and in October of 1967 flight tests were completed.

The BUSHMASTER 2000, according to a company brochure, has all the basic ruggedness of the original Ford trimotor. It has all-metal construction, consisting of new, lighter and stronger corrugated aluminum skins riveted to the flanges of structural members. The wing contains three main spars with five auxiliary spars to reinforce the corrugated skin.

"What we have here," says Ralph Williams, "is a plane designed to be a work-

FORD TRI-MOTORS EXISTING IN 1968

c/n	Reg.	Model	Owner
5-AT-39	N9683	5-AT-B	American Airlines, New York City, N.Y.
5-AT-74	N414H	5-AT-C	American Airlines, New York City, N.Y.
4-AT-15	N4542	4-AT-B	Henry Ford Museum, Dearborn, Mich.
4-AT-69	N8407	4-AT-E	Ford Trimotor, Inc., Ottawa, Kansas
4-AT-10	N6077C	4-AT-A	Eugene Frank, Caldwell, Idaho
5-AT-8	N58996	5-AT-B	Bill Harrah, Reno, Nevada
4-AT-38	N7584	4-AT-B	Island Airlines, Port Clinton, Ohio
4-AT-42	N7684	4-AT-B	Island Airlines, Port Clinton, Ohio
5-AT-11	N1629M	5-AT-B	Island Airlines, Port Clinton, Phio
4-AT-55	N9612	4-AT-E	Johnson Flying Service, Missoula, Montana
4-AT-46	N7861	4-AT-E	Johnson Flying Service, Missoula, Montana
5-AT-34	N9651	5-AT-B	Gaylord Moxon, Santa Monica, Calif.

horse. Capable of take-off, cruise or landing on any two of its three engines. The ability to take-off or land fully loaded in six hundred feet, the length of two football fields . . designed to be equipped with floats, skis, or combinations for specialized requirements."

The fact remains THE BUSHMASTER 2000 is still a Ford Trimotor; the "Tin Goose" simply refused to die.

By February, 1968, THE BUSHMASTER 2000 had logged more than 50 hours of flying and was already sold to a big U. S. corporation.

Meanwhile, there were hundreds of inquiries from all over the world wanting particulars about the plane. Several countries in South America sent delegations to see flight demonstrations. The U. S. Forestry Service expressed interest. So did the U. S. Army, hinting there might be a place for the plane in Viet Nam.

Crack test pilot Bill Bridgeman — "There may be another flying Ford in our future."

Old Henry would like that.

END OF THE DAY. One of Island Airlines Ford trimotors takes off just before sunset for last trip of the day to Put-In-Bay. The "Tin Goose," it seems, just flies on and on and on.   (Island Airlines Photo)

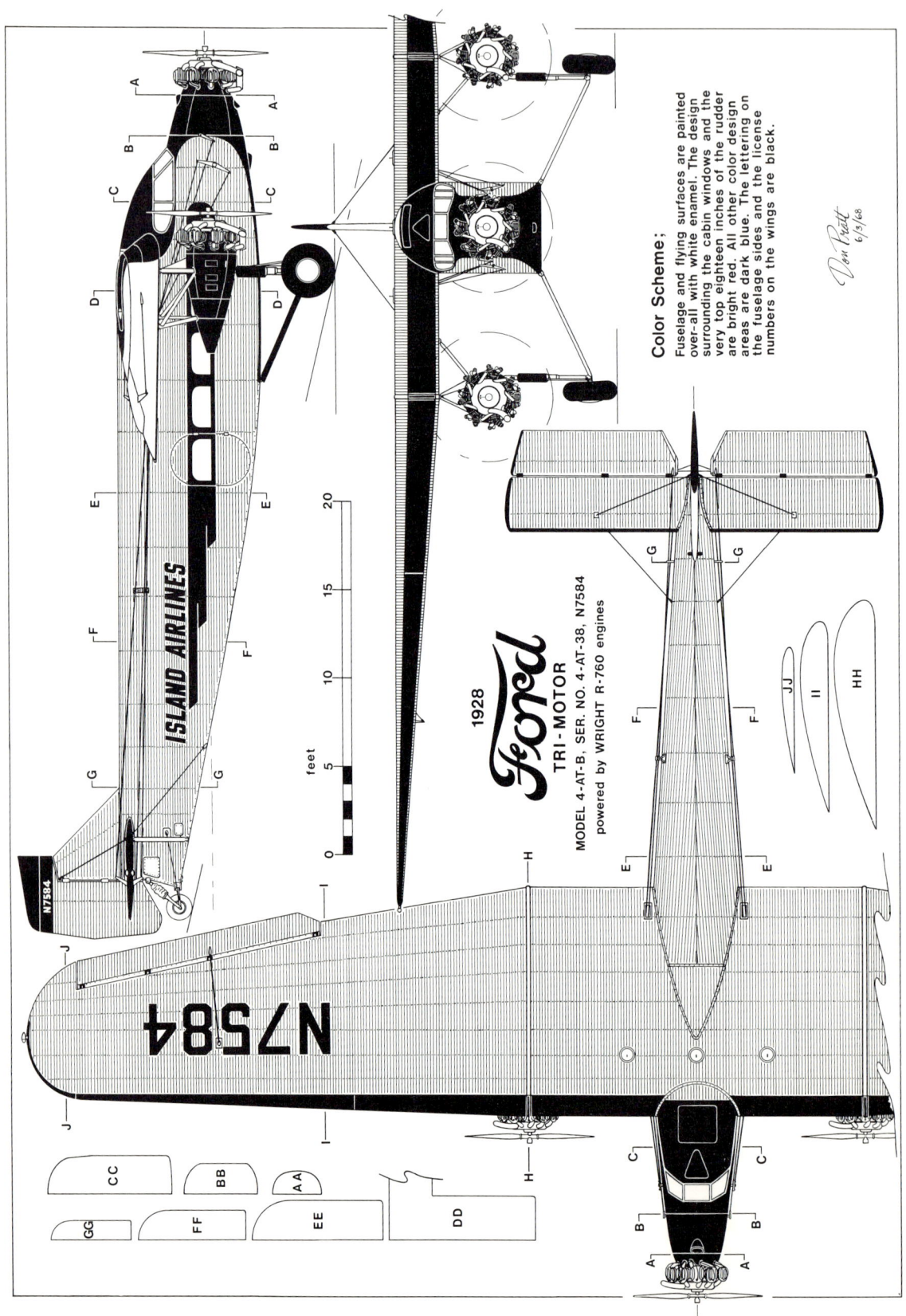

Index

Acosta, Bert, 12
Aerial Age Magazine, 10
"Aerial Sedan," 9, 14
"Aero Cars," 48
Air Mail Act, 22, 46
Air Mail, U.S., 9, 22, 23
"Air Pullman," 15, 16, 17, 24, 25, 26, 27, 38
"Air Sedan," 13, 14, 27
"Air Transport," 17, 19, 21, 23, 24, 26, 27
Aircraft Development Corporation, 16
Aircraft Hydro-Forming Corp., 90, 91
Alaskan Airlines, 79
Alcan highway, 79
"Alclad," 28
American Airways, 46, 86, 87,
American Airlines, Inc., 86, 87, 91
Amundsen, Roald, 45
Army Air Corps, 14, 34, 41, 53, 93
Autogiro, 13
Aviation Hall Of Fame, 27
Aviation Mfg. Corp. (AMCO) 87
Aviation Magazine, 53
Balchen, Bernt, 45
"Barnstormer," 57, 70
"Bat," 10, 11, 12
"Bat Wing," 10, 11
Blue Hole, Castalia, Ohio, 70
Boeing Airplane Company, 53
Boeing Planes:
    Model-247, 55, 56, 67, 71, 72, 78
    Model-727, 59
Boker, Heinz, M.D., 73
Boise (Idaho) 80
Boyer, Joseph, 13
Bridgeman, Bill, 92, 93
Brooks, Harry, 34
Buhl, Arthur, H., 13
Burford, Dean, 23
Burris, Mrs. Dorothy, 65
Bushmaster 2000, 86, 89-93
Busch, Charles, Mrs., 63
Bushnell, David, 9
Byrd, Richard E., 26, 45
Caldwell (Idaho), 79
Cantilever Wing, 10, 37
Campbell, Ed, 45
Catalina Channel Airlines, 92
Cedar Point Amusement Pier, 70
Champion, Albert, 13
Champion Spark Plug Company, 10
Chang Hsueh-Liang, Marshal, 52
Chapin, Roy D., 13
Chrysler, Walter P., 13
Claxton, E. L., 13
Clover Field, Santa Monica, 79
Coffin, Howard, 10
Collings, John, 56
Colonial Air Transport Inc., 87
Consolidated Aircraft Corp., 34
Contract Air Mail Routes:
    CAM-6, 23
    CAM-7, 23
Convair 440, 85
Cugnot, Nicholas, 19
Curtiss, Glenn, 10
Curtiss OX-5 Engine, 13
Curtiss Planes:
    "Carrier Pigeon," 33
    P-40 Pursuit, 34
    Robin, 79
Dearborn Country Club, 20
Dearborn, Michigan, 13
DeHaviland (DH-4), 10, 20
DeLong, Capt. L. S. "Deke," 85
DeValos, Carlos, 87
Dickson, Jim, 68

Dietrick, Ralph, 59, 61, 65, 68, 71, 72, 73. 74, 75, 76, 77, 83
Douglas Aircraft Company, 53
Douglas Planes:
    DC-1 — 48, 49
    DC-2 — 55
    DC-3 — 55, 85, 87
    DC-6 — 85
Dodge, Horace E., 13
Dow, Alex, 13
Duryea, 19
Eastern Air Transport, 46
Eastern Air Lines, 22
Edison, Thomas A., 23
Edsel Ford Trophy, 32
Everitt, B. F., 13
Fair, Roger, 68
Fairchild, 21, 79
Federal Aviation Agency (FAA), 55
Ferguson, William E. 62
Field, Marshall, 13
Firestone, Harvey, 13
Fisher Brothers, 13
Fleet, Ruben, 34
"Flight Escort," 22, 55
"Floyd Bennett," 44, 45
Flying Tigers, 57
"Flying Flivver," 33, 34, 51
Fokker, Anthony H. G., 26
Fokker (Planes) 26, 33, 48
Ford Airport, 21, 23, 24, 31, 33, 42, 53, 57
Ford Air Transport Service, 22, 23, 24, 31, 55
Ford, Edsel B., 9, 13, 14, 16, 19, 20, 22, 25, 32, 33
Ford, Henry, 9, 13, 14, 15, 16, 17, 19, 20, 21, 22, 23, 24, 25, 26, 27, 28, 31, 32, 33, 34, 35, 37, 38, 39, 40, 53, 55
Ford Laboratory, 21, 25
Ford Motor Company, 9, 17, 19, 20, 24, 26, 27, 32, 40, 53
Ford News, 16, 21
Ford Planes:
    2-AT — 17, 21, 14
    3-AT — 17, 24, 25
    4-AT — 26, 27, 37, 40, 41, 42, 46, 50, 52, 65, 67, 78, 83
    5-AT — 45, 46, 50, 52, 56, 65, 67, 70, 78, 79, 85, 87
    14-AT — 53, 55
    Navy (RJ's), 53
    Army (C-9), 41, 53, 57
    Army Bomber (XB-906), 53
Ford Reliability Air Tour, 32, 33
Ford Trimotor, 17, 25, 26, 28, 33, 34, 35, 37, 38, 42, 46, 48, 50, 52, 53, 55, 57, 59, 62, 65, 67, 70, 72
Ford Trimotor, Inc., 83
Frank, Eugene, 79
Glidden Tours, 32
General Motors Corp., 13
Glover, W. Irving, 23
Grand Canyon Airlines, 42, 80
Graceful, 79
Hamilton Standard, 55
Harrah's Automobile Collection, 80, 81
Hauck, Harold, 65
Hayden Aircraft Corp. 87, 90
Hayden, Robert E., 86, 90
Hershberger, Milton, 65, 77
Hicks, Harold, 25, 26
Hispano-Suiza Engine, 10, 14, 55
Hitler, Adolph, 35
Holley, Earl, 13
"Horseless Carriage," 19, 32
Hughes, Jack, 83
Idlewild Airport, 85
Island Airlines, 59, 62, 65, 67, 69, 70, 72, 73, 74, 75, 77, 78, 83, 84, 94
Island Airways, 57, 65
Johnson Flying Service 82, 83, 85, 87
Johnson, Harold, 57

Johnson, Robert R. "Bob," 82, 83
Junkers Aircraft Co., 10
Kennedy International Airport, 85
Kennedy, George C., Gen., 57
Kettering, C. F., 13
Kimm, Capt. Joe., 85
Kirkpatrick, Ross, 23
Kitty Hawk, N. C., 19
Knudsen, William S., 13
Koppen, Otto, 26
Krebbs, 19
Lake Erie, 57, 59, 61, 69
Landa, Torres, 80
Lanley, Bob, 82
Lee, John. 26
Lees, Walter, 15
Lenoir, Etienne, 19
Lent, Irene, 73
Lewis, Rodney, 68, 76
"Liberator" B-24, 34, 35
Liberty Engine, 10, 13, 17, 20, 21
Lighter-Than-Aircraft, 31
Lindbergh, Charles A., 21, 32, 33, 41, 42, 46
Little America, 45
Lockheed Vega, 79
Lonz, George, 62
"Los Angeles" Dirigible, 31
Los Angeles Intl. Airport, 84
McDonnell Douglas Aircraft Co., 26
McDonnell, James, 26
McGraw Hill, 53
Macauley, Alvan, 10
Maddux Airlines, 41, 42
Maddux, Jack, 42
"Maiden Dearborn I," 21
Manning, LeRoy, 53
Marshall, Jack, 68
Martin, Harriet, 72, 73
Martin (Planes), 33
Massachusetts Institute of Technology (MIT), 15, 16
Mattox, Larry, 68
Mayo, William B., 16, 24, 25
Messer, Henry, 87
Mexico, 80, 83
Metzger, W. E., 13
Middle Bass Island, 62, 69, 73, 74
Missoulian Sentinel, 82
Model-T, 9, 16, 19, 20, 28, 31, 38, 42, 48, 50, 75
Monarch Foods, 52
Mott, C. S., 13
Mox-Air, 79
Moxon Electronics Corp., 79
Moxon, Gaylord, 79, 80
Nash, Charlie W., 10
National Advisory Committee For Aeronautics (NACA), 50
National Air Races, 15, 57
National Air Transport (NAT), 40, 80
North Bass Island, 65
Northwest Airways, 46
Navy, U. S., 12, 31, 40, 53
New, Harry S., 23
Nicaragua, 80, 87
North Pole, 26, 45
Northwest Agricultural Aviation, 87
Northwest Airways, Inc., 85, 87
Northwest Orient Airlines, 85
N-414H, 85
N-1124N, 87
N-7584, 84
N-8419, 85
N-9651, 79
N-9683, 86, 87, 90, 91
N-9645, 80
Olds, R. E., 13
Ottawa (Kansas), 83
Packard Motor Car Company, 10
Pan American Airways, 46
Pan American Grace Airways, 42
Perry, Oliver Hazard, 61, 69, 76

Pitcairn, Harold, 13
Poe, Edgar Allen, 17
Polk, R. L., 13
Port Clinton, 57, 58, 59, 65, 70, 73, 74, 76, 77, 78, 84
Post Office Department, 15, 22
Pratt & Whitney, 34, 45, 89, 92
Put-In-Bay, 61, 62, 68, 69, 74, 93
Radio Corp. of America, 79
Rand, Marcell N., 41
Rattlesnake Island, 58, 62, 83, 77
Rockne, Knute, 48
Roosevelt, FDR, 34
Royal Australian Air Force (R.A.A.F.), 56
Royal Typewriter Co., 41, 52
Sandusky, O., 58, 65, 76
Savard, Laurent "Frenchy," 90, 91
Scenic Airways, 42
Schroeder, R. W., 24, 25, 27
Scripps-Booth Motor Co., 10
Seldon, George, 19
Selfridge Field, 14, 15
Servicios Aeronauticos de Mexico, 80
Skytel, 61, 68
Sky Tours, Inc., 67, 68, 72
Smith, James, 19
smooth-skinned Ford, 80, 81
"So Away I Went," 27
South Bass Island, 59, 70, 71
Southwest Air Fast Express (SAFE), 87
"Spirit Of St. Louis," 41
Stair, E. D., 13
Standard biplane, 79
Standard Oil Company, 41
Stinson, Eddie, 15
Stout Engineering Laboratories, 10
Stout Air Service, 41, 42
Stout Metal Airplane Company, 13, 14, 16, 21, 23, 25
Stout, William B., 9, 10, 12, 14, 15, 16, 17, 19, 20, 21, 22, 23, 24, 25, 26, 27, 38, 42, 90
Stranahan, R. L., 10
Sundance fire, 82
"Swallow," 33
Theisen, William, 19
"The Josephine Ford," 26, 45
"Tin Goose," 17, 25, 26, 27, 34, 37, 40, 41, 42, 45, 46, 48, 50, 52, 53, 55, 56, 57, 59, 60, 61, 62, 65, 70, 75, 77
"Tin Goose Flying Club," 70
"Tin Lizzy," 39
Towle, Tom, 25, 26
Traffic Control System, 31
Transportes Aero Centro-Americanos (TACA), 56, 87
Transcontinental Air Transport (TAT), 46, 48, 79, 80, 84
Trans World Airlines (TWA), 48, 53, 56, 79, 80, 84
"Travelair," 33
Tribune, Chicago, 10
Tulsa, Okla., 85
United Air Lines, 40
U. S. Forestry Service, 82, 93
U. S. Weather Bureau, 31
Van Auken, Charles, 19, 20
Vincent, J. G., 13
"Waco," 33, 65
Waltermire, Robt. W., 87
Warner, E. P., 15
Williams, Ralph, 90, 91, 92
Willow Run, 34, 35
Witte, Newell, 68, 75, 76
Wood, Gar, 13, 34
World War I, 20, 26
World War II, 10, 34, 47, 77
Wrigley, P. K., 13
Wright Brothers, 19, 20
Wright Engines, 17, 24, 37
Wright Field, 34
XB-906, 53
XB-NET, 80
"Yackey Sport," 33
Yerex, Lowell, 56
Zilles, Ed, 68
Zuniga, Miguel A., 87